With the Bengal Tigers in the Crimea

With the Bengal Tigers in the Crimea

Recollections of a Soldier of the
17th Leicestershire Regiment
During the Victorian Age

James O'Malley

LEONAUR

With the Bengal Tigers in the Crimea
Recollections of a Soldier of the 17th Leicestershire Regiment During the Victorian Age
by James O'Malley

First published under the title
The Life of James O'Malley

Leonaur is an imprint of Oakpast Ltd

Copyright in this form © 2012 Oakpast Ltd

ISBN: 978-0-85706-980-1 (hardcover)
ISBN: 978-0-85706-981-8 (softcover)

http://www.leonaur.com

Publisher's Notes

The views expressed in this book are not necessarily
those of the publisher.

Contents

Preface

In presenting this, the history of my life, to the public, I may as well say at the outset, that I do not put it forward as a work of literary merit, but as a narrative that can be read and I trust understood by others than those who have received a classical education. I am now passed middle age, and anyone who knows what the condition of the middling class in Ireland was, some fifty years ago, (as at time of first publication), may form some conception of the amount of schooling I had the chance to obtain. Still I have hopes that some amusement, combined with instruction may be found contained in the following pages. I have to thank my dear old comrade the late Thos. Faughnan, for some valuable assistance, without which perhaps more than one incident herein contained would have been imperfectly remembered or it might be forgotten altogether.

Someone once said: "*Any man over forty years should be his own doctor.*" Be this as it may, I am of opinion that no man under that age, should undertake to be his own biographer, but being as I have said on the downward side of the hill of life, I may take it, that my career of a soldier being ended, the only part of my existence likely to interest the public has been passed, and I therefore feel justified in offering them these memoirs. Many of the incidents described, are known to myself. Nobody but those who have been in the battle, can form any opinion of how little any individual knows of what is going on around him, except just in his immediate vicinity, consequently if any one particular attack were described by say half a dozen men, each description would differ widely from the others as probably no two men would have the same experience even in the same battle, although they might be separated by only a few yards during the action.

If I appear sometimes egotistical, please do not imagine I am claiming any special reward for good deeds. I have always endeavoured to do my duty as a British soldier, and although I have, like others, often been in places of great danger, it has pleased God to spare me. I do not pretend to have the powers of a dramatist, to present the various incidents and situations of the campaign before you in such a manner as to cause them to appear other than as an imperfect picture, for I hold that to fully realize a battle field, it must be seen; any description of its horrors will necessarily fall short of the reality, no matter how minutely described.

I trust however that those who do me the favour of perusing the following pages, will find that I have omitted no incident of importance that occurred during my period of service in the Crimea and I can only say that I am in hopes, the very, homely style in which this book is written and absence of any high-flown language, may cause it to find favour, and prove a passport to every heart around which a soldier's life and varied experience may be found interesting.

James O'Malley.

Montreal, April 1893.

Addenda:—

The Leicester Regiment.—Regimental district, No. 17, Leicester Royal Bengal Tigers.—Louisbourg, Hindoustan, Afghanistan, Ghuznee, Khelat, Sebastapool, Ali Masyid, Afghanistan, 1878-79.
Scarlet uniform, lily white facings.

I certify that I have known the bearer, Mr. James O'Malley, since the year 1851, when he enlisted for the 17th Regiment at Galway, Ireland. He served over 10 years therein at Galway, Dublin, Templemore and Cork; 7 months at Gibraltar and 17 months in the Crimea, and was present at the siege of Sebastopol, from 2nd December 1854 to 8th September 1855, including the assaults on the Great Redan on the 18th June and 8th September and of the capture of that city and fortress in the latter date. He was the first man of the regiment wounded in the trenches before Sebastopol. He was also present with the 3rd Brigade of the 4th division which accompanied the English and French fleets to Odessa in Oct. 1855 and was present at the bombardment and surrender of the fortress of Kinburn, 17th Oct. He was at that time one of the smartest men in the Grenadier Company and after leaving the Crimea and landing at Quebec was promoted to corporal in charge of the Regimental Police, which position he held until his discharge from the service He always bore an exceptionally good character in the regiment and left as corporal and in possession of 2 badges for good conduct.

(Signed) John Snasdell,
formerly Colour Sergeant,
17th Regiment.

20 Champlain Street,
Montreal.
22nd February, 1893.

THE CRIMEAN WAR

Then from Balaklava to the front we go
The Chersonese are covered with mud and snow.
Their horses and mules with the Tusks have struck
Transporting provisions for our British pluck.

Tents are blown down with the furious blast,
And rain pours down immensely fast,
The shivering soldier in the trenches stood
With his dripping clothes to chill his blood.

The noble officer brought up with care
In his wet, dismal tent, without dread or fear,
Or a covering party, with their rifles in hand
Marching to the trenches,—a melancholy band.

Or when in camp without fire or mill
To roast our coffee or grind it, still
The Commissariat, to economize expense.
Issued green coffee to show their sense.

To roast and grind as best we could,
Though issuing neither mill nor wood.
Our lines of soldiers, marching rank entire,
Bearing shot and shell, too, at the Russian's fire.

O'er the distant Cossack o'er the hill doth glow,
As winter wraps the Tchernaya valley with snow,
Prince Menchickoff in the Great Redan he stood.
Giving the Muscovites orders to shed our blood.

And General Wyndham on Cathcart's Hill
Giving forth orders to his gallant men;
Yonder the British navy riding in the gale
Anxiously awaiting orders to set sail.

I Join the Royal Bengal Tigers

When I was young, I had a notion that I would like to join the army and be a soldier to fight for the honour and glory of my queen and country. I had frequently seen splendid, well-proportioned, brave-looking soldiers, gaily dressed, marching in Galway, with the band in front of the regiment, discoursing sweet music, which thrilled my soul with a feeling of enchantment. I used to march after them, keeping time to the music until they reached the Castle Barracks, and I made up my mind to enlist as a soldier. One day my attention was directed to a crowd on the green in Galway, around a recruiting party, under the command of a tall sergeant of prepossessing appearance, gaily dressed in a scarlet uniform.

From his neat jaunty little forage cap, (which sat on three hairs) a bunch of gay coloured ribbons floated in the air, and, by his side, his brass mounted polished sword dangled against his heels. The corporal and privates with him, were also tall and well proportioned young fellows; dressed like the sergeant only not quite so expensively. Proudly did they march through the streets; gay and independent as the Roman warriors of old. The sergeant with his penetrating eye and determined countenance, softened with a cheerful look and pleasant smile, winning admiration as he glanced upwards at the windows filled with handsome young maidens and children, who looked on from their elevated positions in wonder and amazement at these noble specimens of the British Army.

"Halt!" cried the sergeant in a commanding tone, which was instinctively obeyed by the party and brought them to a standstill in the middle of the street Here the sergeant took the opportunity of giving a vivid picture of military life. Of its good pay, splendid uniforms, first class rations, and noble discharge. When speaking of campaigns, battlefields, long marches, and forlorn hopes, (the hard vicissitudes of martial life), he declaimed like one who knew something of the terrible drama of war and all its horrors, in which soldiers are the principal actors.

"We want able bodied men," continued the sergeant, "of fine limb and martial appearance, from five feet eight upwards and from 18 to 25 years of age, with good characters free from any disease, blemish or impediments, fit to work at a fortress, throw up earthworks, dig trenches, haul big guns into position, and possessing courage enough to mount the scaling ladders or citadel, fight single handed with the Indians, capture the sword of the *Czar* or the Great Mogul himself, when called upon so to do. I want no lubbers mind, but strong, gallant fellows with heroic minds and any amount of endurance; ready to volunteer for the greatest danger or to go anywhere. To freeze to death in Northern Russia or to simmer on the burning sands of the Sahara desert."

Then followed an oration about glory, blood-money, prize- money and beer-money, medals campaigning, etc, likewise commissions, which was wound up with an exciting invitation to all the young fellows around to join him. "Now", boys, who'll enlist for this and a great deal more? You'll get double pay, double clothing, tools for nothing, superior bedding of long feathers, and three square meals a day. Two holidays a week, a pair of trousers, and two pairs of boots a year. You'll be taught everything in the army and made as straight as a tent pole.

"The humps will be taken off your backs by a pair of loaded clubs, which you'll swing for an hour before breakfast, every morning, in order to sharpen your appetites for that luxurious meal. And here boys I may tell you that you are at liberty to have all the luxuries of the season at that meal if you can pay for them. You'll be taught to turn properly on your heels and toes, and to stand as stiff as starch. You'll be taught the march of intellect and several other marches. The goose step, balance step, front step, back step, side step, quick step and slow step. The running step, the jumping step and to step before the commanding officer in case you misbehave, and from there to step into the Black Hole, if you don't act as becomes a soldier and a gentleman. Now, boys, I am ready to enlist as many as like on the conditions I have specified and treat you as gentlemen.

"There is no compulsion mind! you must all be free and willing! Remember that the corps I am enlisting for, is amongst the bravest and most honourable in the service; with the best officers to be found in the British Army. I hold Her Majesty's commission to enlist for the 17th Regiment, The Leicestershire Royal Bengal Tigers, Scarlet uniforms, lily white facings.

"Now! Gentlemen, select this choice corps. For young fellows, who can do nothing better, it holds out the following inducements, it is a noble profession, it creates ambition, gives opportunity for distinction as well as due credit to genius and leads through valour, and duty faithfully performed to promotion and honour. Heroes are not found amongst peasants but in the army rustics may, and often do, achieve fame far beyond what they might suppose possible. For such young men as you the service is the proper place; where you can make a fortune in a few years, and may be, win your swords and spurs, as many a noble fellow has done before and as any one of you can do if you are so minded. Hurrah! ! Hurrah!!"

The queen was cheered and blessed, and the sergeant was besieged by applicants, ready to take the queen's shilling. After he had performed the solemn ceremony of enlisting a half dozen country fellows I myself stepped boldly up and said "Sergeant I wish to enlist in the 17th Regiment."

"Bravo!" shouted the sergeant "you are just the young lad I want for that gallant regiment. Upon my reputation there is not a gentleman in the three kingdoms does me greater honour than yourself by selecting the Royal Bengal Tigers for your future career. I have not the slightest doubt but that you will be one of the best and bravest soldiers and attain the highest rung in the ladder of promotion."

He then told me to hold out my hand, and answer the following questions:

"Are you free, able, and willing to serve Her Majesty, Queen Victoria, her heirs and successors for a period of 10 years or until you are legally discharged?"

I answered, "I am."

The customary ceremony on such occasions was then gone through in a manner that did credit to the sergeant. The significant shilling was placed in my hand "*in the name of the queen,*" binding me irrevocably to Her Majesty's Service and as an addition to the 17th Regiment. The ribbons were affixed to my hat by the gallant sergeant who marched me and six others before the doctor, who approved of our appearance and before whom we subsequently passed satisfactorily. Here I may say incidentally that I have never had cause to regret joining Her Majesty's Service. The morning following my enlistment, the sergeant took me and the others before a magistrate at 10 o'clock and we were sworn in, after which each received half-a-crown called swearing in money.

Probably few happier groups of young fellows could be encountered than that of which I was one. Laughter and good stories were the rule to which (particularly, the latter) the sergeant contributed no small share. Of the many battles which he described, none made such an impression on my mind as his description of the Battle of "Waterloo" in which he was an active participant. As the description given in his own words (as nearly as my memory will bear me out) may interest my readers, I will endeavour to produce the story here, *verbatim*.

CHAPTER 2

The Segeant's Story of Waterloo

Before commencing, he took a long pull at his canteen, which was slung by a leather strap at his side. The smack of his lips and his jolly manners impressed me with the belief that the canteen contained something stronger and more to his taste than "*Adam's ale*" Fortifying himself still further with a pinch of snuff he said: "On the 18th of June 1815, when Napoléon had formed his line of battle, his brother Jerome commanded on the left, Marshals Soult, and Ney, acted as lieut.-generals to the emperor. The French forces in the field consisted of 80,000 men: the British Army not exceeding that number. Each was commanded by the chief under whom they were prepared to conquer the world, and to whom, each believed defeat an absolute impossibility. So far as the leaders themselves were concerned, they were nearly on an equality as respects military tactics, courage and experience.

The Duke of Wellington had caused the British Army to be formed into two lines, the cavalry being stationed in the rear and distributed along them, but was chiefly concentrated in the immediate rear of the centre: the whole British position in fact formed a sort of curve, or more properly speaking a *wedge*, the centre of which was nearest to the enemy. The plans of the two great leaders were very simple but gave evidence of the fact that the military genius attributed to each of them by the world at large, was not confined to mere theory. The morning broke heavily, but the day although stormy at first ultimately turned out tolerable, fine.

Soon after 10 o'clock, some great agitation was observed in the French lines. Mounted officers were seen galloping with orders from Napoléon in various directions. Shortly before noon the battle commenced in earnest with a cannonade from the French troops, followed by a fierce attack under Jerome Bonaparte, on the advanced post of Hougemont. A crowd of *voltigeurs* preceded the column, and the Naseau soldiers in the wood, were driven back. The assailants encompassed the house of the Hougemont on three sides, and made the most desperate attempts to enter, but a detachment of the British Guards who occupied the villa defended it, and from the loopholed walls and garden, poured upon the French so severe a fire, that the ground was covered with their slain and wounded.

Fresh British troops were now sent to the relief of this post and after severe loss the Coldstream Guards effectually disposed the enemy and took possession. This, however, by no means stopped the fighting as assaults were made upon it again and again, but in the end the French were repulsed, and put to the rout at the point of the bayonet. Not long after the roof was set on fire by the shells of the French batteries, yet the combat was heroically maintained and from the now battle-begrimed walls, a constant and deadly stream of musketry poured forth. Whilst this scene of carnage was being enacted, the whole of the French guns kept up an incessant fire upon the British lines whose guns by no means slow to return the compliment, soon succeeded in silencing many of those of their opponents: the advanced batteries using both shot and shell, causing dreadful havoc amongst the French columns.

Napoléon, under cover of his big guns, ordered a formidable attack upon the left centre. It took all the firmness, prowess and bravery of the British to withstand the shock, although they were formed in that impregnable position known as "*squares*." The distance between the battalions afforded sufficient room to deploy into line, when ordered to do so, consequently the appearance of the battalions from a birds-eye view resembled the chequered squares of a chess board, so that when a squadron of the enemy's cavalry charged between squares, they were exposed at once to a fire in front, from the squares in the rear and to volleys upon both flanks. During the day the French cavalry often experienced the effect of these combined fires. As the French column came up General Kempt Cole, one of the Lords of Cole of Inniskillen, (one of the bravest men that ever wore a sword,) advanced against it with but three British regiments in line and poured in a terrible volley following this up with the true British charge that has made so many of England's enemies quake with fear.

At the same time Pack's brigade bore down upon the right division of this column with the bayonet. The French who had gained the crest of the position, could not stand the British onslaught and after delivering their fire, were forced to beat a hasty retreat.

England, however, sustained a great loss by the death of Picton, who fell in the engagement, a musket ball having passed through his shoulder blade and from thence to his heart. At this moment, the British cavalry made such an effective charge upon the flank of the French column, at the time when they were staggering under the effects of the previous assaults, that they broke the column and compelled them to retreat with great slaughter. On this occasion the British took not only 350 prisoners, but two eagles from the enemy. The prisoners were sent to Brussels as the first fruits of British success. But our cavalry pushing their advantage too far, were met by a strong body of *cuirassiers*, on one flank and lancers on the other, and having charged up to the enemy's guns (which covered the attacking columns) and cut down the gunners, were forced to retire cutting off an angular portion in their retreat.

This movement was however dearly purchased by the death of their commander, but his brigade avenged him so well, that almost the whole of the Polish lancers were cut to pieces, before the strife terminated. Napoléon still persisted in obstinate attacks, and his infantry columns advanced, supported by a division of *cuirassiers*., Opposed to these were the British brigade of heavy cavalry, a corps that has ever done England "Yeoman's Service;" Their meeting was worthy of the ancient Roman arena, as they fought, not at long range like the modern mode of warfare, but sword to sword; desperate blows and passes being exchanged. But notwithstanding the weight and armour of the *cuirassiers* the power of their horses and the undoubted courage of their riders, they could not stand the shock, but were ridden down in masses.

Probably this was one of the fiercest and closest cavalry fights that was ever witnessed, and ended in several hundreds of the French being driven headlong over a deep gravel pit, in a confused mixture of men and horses, exposed to a close fire, which quickly ended their sufferings. One good effect of this impetuous British charge was to cause the enemy to pause, but only to be followed by a more furious onslaught of fresh squadrons. Napoléon exhausted his energies in fierce attacks both horse and foot, relying upon his artillery for support; 250 guns keeping up a constant fire upon the allied position, this fire was so destructive, that the "Iron Duke" directed his troops to retire beyond the exposed ridge and lie down on the ground, until on the near advance of the enemy's horse, they were ordered to stand up in squares advance, meet and repel their charge. Nothing dismayed the French cavalry repeatedly charged the very centre of our position column, following column like the waves of the sea. Vain and useless was their devotion to their cause and country as they came up time and again to break the British square, only to retire with great loss. Their defeat as they were forced back by the deadly vollies, caused them to assume the appearance of a heavy sea pouring itself upon a chain of rocks, which was continually driving it back.

Amidst all the tumult of that desperate action, the discharge of artillery the clash of arms the shouts of the infuriated combatants, the groans and shrieks of the wounded, and dying, the British remained cool and determined, thus causing their bravery to shine with the greatest lustre. In vain did desperate heroes amongst the French cavalry, discharge their firearms at those solid squares in order to compel them to break ranks. They regarded nothing but the actual charge and waited for the word of command to repel the squadrons by their musketry. In vain did the *cuirassiers* ride round and round the bristling walls of steel watching for an opening. Cut and thrust as desperately as they might at the men, or stand and gaze till shot down, the end was practically the same. In vain did the most formidable artillery, literally plough furrows throughout the ranks of the squares.

As the men dropped they were promptly replaced by others: their comrades always being ready to fill up the vacant places, and the fronts remained unbroken. Never did the French make more desperate efforts. They simply courted destruction and more than once did their cavalry seize for a moment the British batteries on the brow of the position.

The cannons were never withdrawn, only the horses were taken to the rear. The gunners did their duty until the last moment and then with their implements took refuge in the nearest squares. When the French were beaten back again, they made haste to re-man their guns and discharged their contents at the retiring foe. Thinned as the artillery of Napoléon had by this time become, the fire kept up by them was incessant, and its formidable discharges were supported by the continuous rolling fire kept up by the whole British line. Notwithstanding the undaunted defence the situation of our army was becoming critical in the extreme.

Wellington had placed his best troops in the front line, these had already suffered severely and the quality of the foreign troops brought to support them proved unequal to the arduous task imposed upon them. The duke himself saw a Belgian regiment waver as it crossed the hill and was on the advance from the second to the first line. Upon which he rode up to them, halted the Regiment and endeavoured to lead them into the fire himself, but all his efforts were in vain and other troops had to replace these "*battle scared*" soldiers. All through the thickest of this blood-shed and carnage, the Duke of Wellington was everywhere (like "bad luck" as one of his soldiers said).

On account of the position of the armies and the nature of the ground, there was scarcely a square which he did not visit, encouraging the men by his presence and stimulating the officers to their duty by his directions. During the hostile charges, he frequently threw himself into the nearest square for protection watching every movement and advance of the enemy and piercing through the smoke with an eagle eye, galloped to every point, however exposed, if it seemed to require his presence. Many of the short phrases he addressed to his troops had a perfectly talismanic effect. Distinguishable as he was by his suite and the movements of his staff who went and came with orders, it is a matter of no little surprise that, like the immortal Nelson, a stray bullet did not lay him low especially as they were falling thickly around him. "That's good practice" he remarked to one of his staff on seeing a bullet just graze the tip of his boot. "I think; that the French are firing better than they did in Spain."

Again, riding up to the 95th regiment when in front of the line and threatened with a formidable charge of cavalry, he said: "Stand fast 95th, we must not be beaten!! What they will say in England?!!!"

On another occasion when brave men were falling very fast, he said with the utmost coolness, "Hard pounding this, but never mind, boys, we'll win the battle yet. Let us see who will pound longest!!"

All who heard him issue orders received fresh confidence from his readiness and cool composure. His staff fell man by man beside him. An *aide-de-camp* was sent with an important message to a brigadier-major. On his return he was shot through the lungs, but borne up by the consciousness of duty to be performed, he rode up to the duke delivered his answer and then *dropped dead* from his horse. And at this time there was no certainty that all this sacrifice had not been made in vain. The French although repulsed on every side persisted in making incessant attacks, and the British squadrons from the constant firing and assaults, presented a diminished and less formidable appearance.

One general officer stated that his brigade had lost one third of its number and that the survivors were so exhausted with fatigue, that a brief respite however short, seemed absolutely necessary. The "Iron" Duke replied, "what you propose is impossible. You and I and every British soldier must die on the spot we now occupy rather than be beaten!!"

"It is enough," replied the general, "I and every man under my command will die or stand to the last!"

All this time the battle was raging fiercely, without any apparent advantage to either side. The frightful contest was maintained along the entire line, with unabated stubbornness and ferocity, the infantry advancing in echelon of squares to meet the advances of the French cavalry, whilst the artillery literally cut up the enemy between the squares as they advanced. The British cavalry were then in reserve, but were prepared to charge and only too eager to get the word to do so. All this time, despite the desperate onslaughts of the French, *not one British square had been broken,* but the enemy had suffered most severely from their rash attempts to cause our men to "run:" a thing unknown to the British soldier. Our ranks however had been thinned by the superior numbers and formidable artillery that had been brought to bear upon them for so many hours.

About half past four, two brigades were brought from Hills' corps on the right, to the left centre, in anticipation of an attack on the weakest part of the position. A slight pause occurred on both sides, owing partly to the fact that both commanders were watching each other's tactics, somewhat uncertain as to what was going to be the next move, or where it was likely to take place. This was only broken by the roar of big guns, and victory seemed still undecided for either side. The crisis of the struggle, however, was at hand. Napoléon was desperate, and resolved to sacrifice his last chance of retreat before the Prussians came up. Although his cavalry were already wrecked, and he had lost besides 17,000 men, his hopes of victory had evidently not left him.

There was no time to be lost for the Prussian guns were beginning to thunder on his flank, to the great delight of Wellington, who cried out in a paroxysm of joy "There goes old Blücher at last!!!" and by the light of the setting sun, his forces were seen issuing from the woods. Napoléon had still some 20,000 men of his faithful guard, who were placed during the action in reserve behind "La Belle Alliance" and had hardly pulled a trigger. Leaving his more remote point of observation on the heights in rear of his line. Napoléon himself led them forward to the foot of the allied position. He then had them defile before him and telling them that the British army was nearly destroyed, and that to carry the position they had only to brave the fire of the artillery, pointing to the causeway he examined, "Gentlemen! there lies the road to Brussels!"

He was answered by loud shouts of "*Vive l'Empereur! Vive l'Empereur!*" which induced the British to believe that Napoléon himself was going to lead the troops in person, to the attack and consequently every eye was directed to that quarter, but owing to the clouds of smoke nothing could be seen distinctly. In the meantime Wellington changed the position of his forces so as to repel the assaults, and two battalions of the Guards were formed into line and marched to the brow of the hill, where they were ordered to lie down. Led by Marshal Ney, the Imperial Guards dauntlessly advanced, rallying as they went, such of the broken cavalry and infantry as yet maintained the conflict. The British line by their successes on the right, had pushed forward and now changed from a convex, to a concave position, so that our artillery raked the French columns as they advanced and, so accurately were the guns directed, that the heads of the columns were constantly cut off.

Borne in, however, by the impetuosity of those in the rear, they at length attained the summit of the ridge where the British lay concealed. At this important moment, Wellington (who had placed himself in the rear of the Guards), when he thought the French were near enough gave the order at the top of his voice: "Up guards and at them!!" They sprang to their feet as if by magic and poured in on the French a well-directed fire which staggered them very considerably. A second volley put them in a sort of panic, and the duke galloping close to their rear cried out: "Forward Guards, charge!!!" and with a ringing hurrah they obeyed and rushing down the hill were upon the French with charged bayonets, causing even that crack regiment the veteran guards of France, the chosen of Napoléon's army to turn tail and fly. The British followed them in fine style and nearly destroyed them.

Ney fought sword in hand even after his horse was shot from under him. His uniform was completely riddled by bullets and he was the last to quit the struggle. Napoléon's last hope was gone, when he saw the flower of his army fly before the impetuous charge of the British troops, but when he saw his cavalry fly and mixing with the fugitives trample them down, he cried "all is lost" then, shook his head and turned as pale as death. Soon after, two bodies of British cavalry rapidly advanced upon either flank and the Prussians were closing up his rear. Now was the time (had Napoléon's spirit dictated it) for him to die a brave warrior's death. But no, he said to his *aide-de- camp* who remained at his side, the fatal words "All is lost! and it is time to save ourselves!!" and putting spurs to his horse, *turned and fled* leaving to their fate the gallant soldiers who had that day shed their blood with such profusion.

Considering that he was looked upon by his army as perfectly invincible, it may well be imagined what an utterly "*routed*" feeling must have prevailed amongst his adherents when his crack regiment turned and fled. Meanwhile the whole British Army, led by the illustrious conqueror himself, charged the French who still maintained the combat, Amidst increasing slaughter, the whole of Napoléon's grand army, fled from the indomitable bravery of the British. As our troops followed up, the French guns had gradually ceased firing, the gunners having abandoned them. The drivers cut the traces of their horses, in order to enable them to fly the quicker. Infantry, cavalry, officers and men, were mixed up in their headlong flight, strewing the ground as they went with their wounded, dead and dying. ,

As they rushed over waggons, arms, and overturned artillery, pursuers and pursued tore madly over all that lay in their path. A slight attempt at resistance was made by four or five battalions of the Old Imperial Guards, who threw themselves into squares and stood firm, but even these tried and heroic fellows were very soon disposed of by the impetuosity of the British. The Allies still continued the pursuit of the flying foe and the once "grand army" of Napoléon was virtually annihilated. The advance on Paris by the victors was made at once and met with but very little opposition. Not long afterwards, Napoléon whilst attempting to escape from the British, was captured and banished to the island of St. Helena, some distance from the Cape of Good Hope, where he died in exile on the 5th May 1821.

As soon as the story was ended, the worthy sergeant refreshed himself from his canteen and smacking his lips as if the draught had done him good (as no doubt it had) said "Now boys to finish up with I will sing you a song" which he did as follows:

The Soldier's Dream.
Our bugle sung truce, for the night-cloud bad lowered,
And the sentinel stars set their watch in the sky,
And thousands had sunk on the ground over powered,—
The weary to sleep, and the wounded to die.

25

When reposing that night on my pallet of straw,
By the wolf-scaring baggot that guarded the slain;
At the dead of the night—a sweet vision I saw,
And twice ere the morning I dreamt it again.

Methought from the battlefield's dreadful array,
Far, far I had roamed on a desolate track,—
T'was autumn, and sunshine arose on the way.
To the home of my fathers, that welcomed me back.

I flew through the pleasant fields, traversed so oft
In life's morning march when my boom was young:
I heard my own mountain goats bleating aloft.
And I knew the sweet strain that the corn reaper sung.

Then pledged me the wine-cup, and fondly, I swore.
From my home and my weeping friend never to part:
My little ones kissed me a thousand times o'er.
And my wife sobbed aloud in her fullness of heart.

"Stay, stay with us—rest I—than art weary and worn!"
And fain was their war-broken soldier to stay;
But sorrow returned with the dawning of mom.
And the voice on my dreaming ear melted away.

At the conclusion of his vocal effort the applause was almost deafening, during which he took the opportunity of filling his pipe and commenced smoking. Whilst thus regaling himself with the fragrant weed, he gave us quite a few wrinkles as to our future behaviour both in and out of the barrack room. I have often thought since, what a benefit it would be to soldiers in general if their enlisting sergeant would only take the pains in the beginning to impress upon the minds of the young recruits the benefits accruing from honest, kindly, and manly behaviour not only when forced, but when any opportunity offered for the display of such qualities. This is precisely what our sergeant did with us, and, I for one, certainly was much struck by the advice so kindly offered and I must say that, I have reason to believe that much of my success whilst in the army was due to my having endeavoured to carry it out in practice.

Men who do what is *right*, very soon find their names, favourably known in the highest quarters and are often surprised to find how quickly their superior officers find out and appreciate their merits. Consequently promotion is frequently very rapid, proving the truth of the old adage "*Virtue is its own reward.*" In fact, if a man really and conscientiously performs his duty, there is no place in the world where he will be better appreciated or where his position will be more quickly benefitted, then in the British Army. All men who have risen above the social level, upon which they were born, have been men ever ready to lend a helping hand to a comrade or even a stranger when it seemed necessary, and did not wait for the word of command to do so. A grudging disposition, that is to say one who stands strictly upon what he is pleased to term his "rights" is pretty sure not only to fail in attaining any promotion, but may even run the chance of being igno-miniously dismissed from the service which can well bear the loss of a fellow who is neither ornamental nor useful in any capacity.

Chapter 3

Army Days in Ireland

The next day we were marched off to the regimental hospital by the orderly corporal where we were made to pass another strict examination before Dr Campbell, to test our soundness as regarded the internal organizations limbs and eyesight. We had to strip, and then walk fast, slow, bend the legs and arms and put the body generally through a variety of difficult manoeuvres. Our eyesight too was subjected to some rigorous tests, after which, being finally declared fit for service, we were marched to the quartermaster's stores and received our uniform and kit which latter consisted of one each of the following articles, *viz*:

Pair of boots	Canteen and cover
Cloth trousers	Knapsack
Summer trousers	Two shirts
Shako	Two pairs socks
Tunic	Two towels (for the
Stock and clasp	marking of which we
Shell jacket	were charged one
Forage cap	halfpenny each)
Pair of mitts	Hold all containing
Tin of Blacking	Knife, fork, spoon,
Pair of braces	razor, shaving brush
Clothes Brush	and comb

We were next taken to the tailor's shop, where we had our clothing altered and fitted. This occupied four or five days, during which time we were exempted from drill, but had to do duty as orderly men by turns. This consisted of cooking the meals of the men on drill etc, keeping the barrack rooms clean and in proper order. When our clothing had been, made to fit us, we then turned out to drill three times a day, *viz*: Before breakfast club drill. 8 a. m., to 9 a. m.: setting up drill. At 10 o'clock the commanding officer's parade. In the afternoon, setting up drill and adjutant's parade which took place at 2 o'clock. At all these drills and parades, we were minutely inspected by the orderly sergeant and afterwards by the sergeant major, when, if the least fault was found with us we were ordered to another parade called the "dirty parade," but I took very good care not to incur the necessity of presenting myself at the latter.

When drill commenced we were formed into squads of eight or ten men each, in line at arm's length apart, termed a "squad with intervals." After drilling in single ranks for a week, one squad was increased to two ranks at open order, the rear rank covering the intervals. The sergeant-major frequently came round to superintend the drills and whenever he found an attentive, deserving, recruit invariably sent him up to a more advanced squad. In this way the more intelligent and deserving recruits were advanced and it gave them great encouragement to persevere still more. I was fortunate enough to be one of the first sent up for promotion and I afterwards progressed step by step until I reached the advanced squad where I was initiated into changing guard, challenging at night, giving and receiving the countersign, receiving rounds grand rounds etc.

Also we were taught manual and platoon exercise, company and battalion movements. We were then put through a course of ball practice the distances being from one hundred and fifty yards gradually increased to four hundred; the old "Brown Bess" being the weapon then in use. I seemed to have quite a lucky star shining over me as I succeeded in making a couple of "Bull's Eyes" beside a number of centres. After we had finished this course, we were again inspected by our musket instructor, before whom we acquitted ourselves very creditably, and to his entire satisfaction. We were then accordingly, dismissed from recruit drill and returned as fit to do duty as soldiers. The principal buildings in Galway are The Queen's College at Newcastle, a really grand and imposing edifice, a great number of monasteries and nunneries, Smith's College, the Court House and barracks, also the grand old church of Saint Nicholas.

Outside of the town of Galway the principal places of note are Sailor's Hill, and Salt Hill but these have been so often described that it would be useless for me to weary the reader with a long description of them. In the town and suburbs, there are numerous flour and other mills, breweries and distilleries.

Extensive salmon and sea-fishing is carried on along the coast. The bay is a large expanse of water about eighteen miles broad at its seaward extremity, diminishing about eight miles inland and being about twenty miles long. It is protected from the swell of the Atlantic by the Arran Isles. South west from Galway to the sea, is the district called Connemara, which contains vast tracts of bog lands, moss loughs, and marshes. These present a bleak and dreary aspect to the stranger. Galway abounds in ancient remains of the Celtic as well as the Norman period. Monastic remains are quite numerous in several parts of the country. One of the finest specimens of this class is that of Knocknoy, near Tuam, besides various other round towers. There was plenty amusement for our officers, shooting, fishing etc., and, they usually managed to return from their expeditions with their creels and game bags well filled. So that there was no lack of trout, salmon, and winged game as well as an occasional hare etc. Besides these enjoyments they managed to get up a dramatic club with Lieutenant Lindsay, Lieutenant Coultherst, Captain McPherson, Captain Grover and Captain Gordon together with some more officers at their head as well as a few smart non-commissioned officers and privates.

The performances were well patronized and not only by the officers and their ladies but by the best and highest in the town, as well as any of the soldiers who cared to attend, making quite an agreeable diversion from the routine of barrack duties.

On the 10th May 1851 my company was ordered to Portumna, under the command of Captain McKenstrie, (He afterwards because colonel of the second battalion, and was stationed in Toronto at the time of the Trent affair). The first day's march was to Oranmore. The second to Loughrea. Whilst there, we were billeted on the different shop keepers in parties of from two to six on each billet. The third day's march we arrived in Portumna, having marched forty miles in three days, carrying a full kit. The country was very beautiful and our officers found plenty amusement shooting and fishing as well as boating on the River Shannon. On the 29th April 1852, we got the route for Dublin, the first day's march being to Birr, King's County. The second day's march was to Kennettoe, Queen's County. The third day we reached Mount Mellick, a remarkably handsome inland town. The fourth days march found us in Minster Evans, in the County Kildare where we were most hospitably received, completing eighty miles of marching, in four days of heavy marching order; rather a trying ordeal for recruits. Of course we were billeted on the shop keepers as before.

On the 5th day, we took the Cork express for Dublin. Arriving at the station we could see Wellington's monument in Phoenix Park. Here we were met by our own regimental band, also the band of the 39th who played us up to Richmond barracks. On arrival we were told off to our respective quarters and dismissed. There are splendid, large, airy barracks sufficient for two regiments, with excellent officer's and staff quarters, but very bad accommodation for married soldiers, who were obliged to rent apartments outside, and live like many of the civilians in tenement houses. This is a great inconvenience to married soldiers which the authorities ought to remedy without further delay, if they have not already done so. The military force in Dublin consisted of the 1st Dragoon Guards stationed in the Royal barracks under command of Lord Cardigan as well as the Scott Greys. The 11th Hussars and the 16th Lancers in Island Bridge barracks. Three batteries of the Royal Artillery were stationed in Portobello. The 17th and 39th were quartered in Richmond barracks. The 27th Enniskillen (now 27 Royal Irish Fusiliers) lay at the Royal barracks as well as the 52nd Light Infantry and 91st Regiment, besides those at the *depôts* at Beggars Bush barracks.

The whole were under the command of Major General, Sir Edward Blakeney, (the commander in-chief of the force in Ireland) whose quarters were situated at The Old Man's Hospital near Phoenix Park. The regiments furnish the garrison duties in their turns daily; the regiment forming the Castle guard, finding the staff colours, etc. The colours are trooped every morning on the esplanade at 10 o'clock when the guards are inspected by the town major and the men marched off to their respective posts. The numbers of the different guards are as follows:

Castle guard, one captain, one subaltern, two sergeants, two corporals, and 27 privates.
Lower Castle, one sergeant, one corporal, and 9 privates.
Vice Regal Lodge, one sergeant, two corporals and 21 privates.
Old Man's Hospital, one sergeant, two corporals and 15 privates.
Kilmainham, one corporal and three privates.
Arbour Hill Hospital, one sergeant, one corporal and 15 privates.

Magazine in the Park, one sergeant, one corporal and 9 privates.

Island Bridge, one sergeant, one corporal and 15 privates.

Bank of Ireland, opposite College Green, one subaltern, one sergeant, one corporal and 15 privates.

Richmond, one sergeant, two corporals and 15 privates.

Mount Joy Guard, one corporal and 8 men.

Relieving the Castle Guard, is one of the most impressive martial ceremonies and invariably attracted large crowds of people to witness it, as well as to enjoy the inspiriting strain of the military bands which discoursed the liveliest music during the performance of this duty. Before the old guard marches off, the new guard plants its colours in the centre of the castle yard with a double sentry over them. Two sentries are posted at the gate of the castle yard, and two on the door of the castle itself, under the portico. All the sentries of the old guard having been relieved, the guard is marched off by its captain, the subaltern carrying the colours: the new guard saluting the old by presenting arms, and then taking the place of the old. The relief being told off, they are dismissed to the guard room.

The guards always take their rations with them, which consists of three-quarters of a pound of beef or mutton, one pound and a half of bread, one pound and a half of potatoes and onions, one eighth of an ounce of tea, a quarter of an ounce of coffee, two ounces of sugar, with pepper and salt to each man. There being only one pot and pan to each guard room, you will readily perceive that they are kept in active use from the time the men mount post in the morning until 6 o'clock in the evening: every relief boiling their potatoes and making tea or coffee as they come off sentry. I was detailed for guard at the Old Man's Hospital, which is a large establishment and consists of the major general's quarters, and the English church, where the troops from Richmond attend divine service as well as the old pensioners. There are quarter's here for about 1000 men.

Any pensioners can be admitted who apply, except married men. They have to pay in their pension for their board and clothes. The latter consists of cloth trousers, red tunic and Napoléon hat. They have no duties to perform, only to keep themselves and their quarters clean and in proper order, and they can live very comfortably. The grounds and kitchen gardens around this institution, show the cleanliness and taste of these old veterans whose home is now found for them by a country grateful to them for their past services in her behalf. Upon being relieved from guard next day, we had "kit inspection" by the commanding officer accompanied by Major Cole who had not long joined the regiment. On Sunday we had church parade at 10 o'clock a. m. and having been inspected, we marched off, the band playing through Kilmainham to the Old Man's Hospital, where the Protestants and Roman Catholics parted for the time being, the latter marching to St Mary's Church on Arran quay.

As we marched alongside the Liffey, the splendid music from the different bands, on their road to church was truly spirit stirring as it re-echoed along the river, and caused a peculiarly pleasant sensation to the feelings, seeming to raise our thoughts heavenward. It is much to be regretted that the practice of having the bands play whilst on the way to church, is not carried out now on Sunday, owing to some foolish puritanical objections. Surely the Almighty has as much right to be praised by good music as the colonel of a regiment. This by the way however.

Strict military discipline, numerous general field days and reviews, drilling at tent pitching in the nine acres field, regimental drills and parades with five nights in bed between guards, kept our men pretty busy, but the beautiful walks in Phoenix Park and drives to the Strawberry beds on side carts with our sweethearts on Sunday afternoons, together with the numerous other amusements such as theatres, concerts, museums, picture galleries and the scenery of everyday life in the city compensated us for the hard duty and strict discipline. On the whole we were therefore well pleased with Dublin as a military station.

CHAPTER 4

Off to Fight the Russians

On the 15th August 1852, I was picked out for the grenadier company and although my h eighth was 5 feet 11 inches. I was the smallest man in the party. At this time an event happened that cast a gloom not only over the entire army but the country generally That grand old warrior The Duke of Wellington whose memory will be always green and whose heroic deeds will remain matters of history standing in relief until the world ceases to be, ended his earthly career at the ripe old age of 84 years. This sad event occurred on Tuesday 14th September 1852, after only a few hours illness at Walmer Castle, his official residence. The mournful intelligence was received with the deepest regret both by the officers and men of our regiment. The hero of St Sebastian, Salamanca, Quatre-Brass, Ligny and Waterloo had at last paid that inevitable penalty which "*all men born of woman*" are sooner or later called upon to pay.

On the 1st of November, a general order was issued directing one officer, one sergeant and 20 rank and file from each regiment then in garrison to proceed on the 8th to London, to take part in the funeral procession of the late field-marshal, His Grace the Duke of Wellington, including Lieutenant Earle, Captain Croker, Sergeant Plant and another, 15 rank and file. (Of which I was selected to be one). We paraded with the other regiments in garrison where we were inspected by the general and marched off with a field officer in charge, embarking on the steamer at the North Wall at 6 p. m. There was on board about 203 picked men from the various corps in Dublin. The men had a very smart soldierly appearance, and altogether, seemed to deem it quite an honour to have been selected for this service.

All being ready the captain called out "All aboard" and immediately afterwards the steamer moved out slowly from her moorings, passing clear of the shipping, and Pigeon House Fort on the right, where several detachments had assembled and who gave us three lusty cheers, such as only British soldiers and sailors know how to give, as the steamer rushed onwards. Soon city and shore were passed and then there was nothing to be seen but sky and water.

Towards night, the clouds looked threatening but darkness closed about us without any bad weather putting in an appearance, although many of the soldiers, never having had experience of the sea, thought we were in for a big storm. But although the steamer rolled and pitched to a degree that to us landsmen was very trying, that was the extent of our misfortune. After a pretty good deal of this kind of movement, (which the sailors only regarded as child's play) we steamed into Liverpool about 6 o'clock a. m. were we disembarked and having got breakfast, marched to the railway station taking the 9 o'clock train for London.

The morning was fair and the train went along at good speed, covering the distance of 180 miles in 5 hours, thus making an average of 40 miles an hour, and arriving at Euston Station on time. Our quarters in London were in Regents Park. The procession on the morning of the 13th of November although necessarily of a melancholy appearance, was most imposing. We had good weather and the troops looked simply splendid. Most of the way from the Chelsea Hospital, where the body had lain in state, right up to St Pauls' Cathedral, the streets were lined on both sides with both cavalry and infantry. Noon sharp the cortege left the hospital escorted by a guard of honour.

The bands played the "Dead March" and minute guns were fired as the procession proceeded on its way to the last earthly resting place of the departed hero, where on arrival the body was lowered into the crypt in close proximity to the corpse of the ever memorable Lord Nelson, waiting for the last trumpet to call the quick and the dead. The funeral was beyond doubt one of the grandest and most solemn that was ever seen before in England or any other country and is probably remembered to this day by some of the soldiers (if still living, as at time of first publication), that took part in it. When all was over, we returned by rail the following morning to Liverpool taking the steamer at 6 p.m. for Dublin where we arrived twelve hours letter *viz* 6 the following morning, after rather a rough passage.

It is the rule to change the regiments stationed in Dublin, from one barracks to another, every 10 months. Ours having put in the regulation time in Richmond, we exchanged with the 63rd from the

Royal barracks. The first of April we marched from our old quarters meeting on our way the 63rd who being the junior regiment, saluted us, the 17th, according to the rule of etiquette in force in the service. On arrival, our quarters were taken up in Valentine Square. We were mightily pleased with this exchange as we were thereby brought closer to the various amusements sights, etc., of the city. Twelve men of each company were now armed with the Enfield Rifle which, although, now considered an obsolete weapon, was at that time a considerable improvement upon the arms carried by us, *viz* the old "Brown Bess." They were ordered to proceed to the Pigeon House fort in order to undergo a. course of instruction in the handling of the rifle, on the beach.

On completion of this course the rifles were handed over to twelve others and so on until the entire brigade had been thoroughly drilled in their use. In the summer of the same year 1853, Dublin was visited by the queen and Prince Albert. A message having been received that the royal party were to land at Kingstown, the grenadiers, and light company were ordered to proceed by rail from Westland Row station to that place to do duty as a guard of honour, leaving the Royal Barrack at 8 a. m., under the command of Captain John Croker, who was killed some time afterwards on the 18th June 1855 in the memorable assault on the Great Redan. Our formation was arranged in such a manner that it left a passage between our two lines for Her Majesty and consort to pass from their yacht, which came alongside the quay; a red carpet having been laid down previously for Their Majesties to walk on, to the railway carriage prepared for their reception and then in waiting.

After standing in position for upwards of an hour or more the royal yacht was at last seen steaming into harbour, at sight of which, the different ships in port, fired a royal salute, whilst from the merchant vessels and people congregated about, deafening cheers arose, testifying to the warm place the queen held in the hearts of her subjects. Plainly visible walking the decks, were Her Majesty and the prince, and both were highly pleased with their enthusiastic reception. Upon arrival the royal party landed without delay and as Her Majesty stepped ashore, the guns of St Georges' battery paid her homage, at the same time the bands broke out with "God save the Queen" most heartily rendered. Their Majesties were then conveyed by special train to Dublin escorted by their guard of honour, where the queen opened the great exhibition at Merrion Square, the special guard of honour

Captain John L Croker, 17th Foot, Crimea

for this occasion being furnished by the 16th Lancers.

On the conclusion of the ceremony they went to the Vice Regal Lodge, accompanied by several troops of cavalry. Some thousands of people flocked to the exhibition to see Their Majesties and the cheering and waving of hats, handkerchiefs and even women's shawls was incessant, all along the route traversed. Both the prince and the queen were much touched, and gracefully acknowledged this heartfelt loyalty of their subjects. At night the whole city was illuminated and grand displays of fireworks were exhibited, flags were flying in all directions and for a time it really seemed as if all the populace had gone wild with joy. College Green, past the Bank of Ireland, up to the castle, along Grafton street as far as Stephen's Green along Merrion Square to the Exhibition buildings, by the post office, along the Liffey up as far as Phoenix Park, every place seemed to vie with the others in making the greatest display of their loyal feelings.

All the troops got leave of absence until 12 o'clock to give them an opportunity of witnessing this grand scene, and everywhere the excitement was intense. Two days afterwards, the troops in garrison were ordered to assemble in review order at 10 a. m., in the Phoenix Park, to be reviewed before Her Majesty and Prince Albert. On the day appointed, the troops were marched to that place, the bands playing at the heads of their respective regiments, thousands of citizens accompanying them, and were at once formed in line of columns facing the chief secretary's Lodge, the field-batteries being on the flanks and the cavalry in the rear. Promptly at 10 a. m., Sir Edward Blakeney and his staff arrived and after an interval of a few minutes deployed the troops into line. The appearance of Her Majesty on the ground was the signal for the artillery to fire a royal salute the infantry meanwhile presenting arms and the bands playing "God save the Queen."

Seated in an open carriage, Her Majesty was then driven slowly down the front of the line inspecting the whole with a lively interest, including the boys of the Hibernian School. After inspection, the troops were marched past in slow, quick, and double time and were then put through various manoeuvres. The queen expressed great pleasure with all she witnessed which so worked upon the feelings of the crowd that a rather ludicrous incident was the consequence. The people made a rush to take out the horses from the carriage in order to draw it themselves. Prince George however mistaking their intention thought it an attempt to assault Her Majesty, not understanding the impulsive warm hearted nature of the Irish, and immediately ordered the cavalry to form up. But on perceiving his mistake, he at once apologised. This caused no little amusement to the queen, who after witnessing the various evolutions including pursuing practice by the hussars, drove away well satisfied with all she had seen, to the Vice Regal Lodge accompanied by a cavalry escort.

According to published official statistics there could not have been less then 80,000 spectators present; a sight never before witnessed in Dublin. The troops were then marched to their different barracks; their bands playing. On arrival at their quarters the grenadiers and light company were detailed as a guard of honour to Her Majesty during her visit to the Vice Regal Lodge, and to be examined in front of the lodge so as to be ready to turn out at Her Majesty's pleasure After she had left Dublin, she visited the Lakes of Killarney, remaining there some days and from thence she went to Queenstown, Cork where she embarked on board her Royal yacht for England. The public buildings of Dublin are deservedly famed for their grandeur and number. Amongst them I may name the Bank of Ireland, (formerly the house of Parliament), the Custom House, Trinity College and the four courts, which have a very imposing appearance.

There are numerous places of worship: Protestant and Roman Catholic, Convents arid a Jewish Synagogue. Perhaps the most re-markable amongst the protestant churches are Christ' Church and St Patrick's Cathedral, and amongst the Roman Catholic St Mary's, St Agustines', St Saviours and St Raven's. Here also are to found monuments of William the third, in College Green, the Duke of Wellington, in the Park and that of Lord Nelson in Sackville street. The public squares are well kept. Stephen's Green occupies an area of about 20 acres and is something like a mile or more in circumference. Merrion Square is considered the most aristocratic whilst Rutland Square with the Rotunda at the end of Sackville Street and Glasnevin on the north deserve attention, being the resting place of Daniel O'Connel, Tom Steele, and Curran. The Phoenix Park, covering as it does very nearly 2,000 acres of land, heavily timbered, is a magnificent sight, and affords plenty of scope for military review. It is also much used by the inhabitants for receptions, etc. The Liffey is spanned by nine bridges; two of which are constructed of iron. The banks of this river are faced with granite walls.

At Christmas our Capt. John Croker treated the company to a barrel of Guiness' XXX Porter: Lieutenants Coulthurst and Earle looking after the sergeants and married men in the way of some substantials to cheer them at that festive season. All the usual decorations of the company's rooms with evergreens, holly, etc , not forgetting the time honoured mistletoe were most tastefully arranged under the immediate supervision of the non-commissioned officers and an enjoyable evening was spent in story-telling, songs, and a "hop" to wind up with. Winter is a pleasant time here and we were not over-burdened with drill. On December the 10th, I obtained leave of absence for four weeks to visit my friends and relations in Galway. When my leave had expired, I got a renewal of two weeks more, but before the two weeks were up, the colonel got orders from the Horse Guards to prepare the regiment for foreign service as it was ordered to Gibraltar, consequently I had to make my *adieus* to my parents and friends.

On the 15th of January I joined the regiment in Ship Street Barracks in Dublin The following day I passed the doctor who declared me fit for foreign service. On the 16th February. 1854, we got the route for Templemore, a town about 100 miles south-west of Dublin. At 10 a. m., after inspection by Colonel McPherson, K. C. B. (who took command of the regiment) we marched to the railway station, the band playing "The British Grenadiers" and "The Girl I left behind me." Thousands of people turned out to see us and cheered lustily as the train left the station, when the band struck up "Auld Lang Syne." We accomplished the distance in three hours and upon arrival at our destination, marched to our respective quarters. These barracks were the same as those at Richmond being quite large enough to accommodate two regiments with ease. The town is small but pleasant being surrounded by some wonderfully pretty country scenery.

We staid in Templemore something over two months when we received orders to proceed to Cork by rail on the 27th April, there to embark on board two sailing transports, the *Dunbar* and *Cornwall*, two sister ships, the right wing going in the latter and the left wing in the former. War with Russia having been declared on Friday 28th March, we believed that, although ordered to Gibraltar, before many months elapsed, we should have the honour and glory of taking the field shoulder to shoulder with those troops who had preceded us to the seat of war in the east. On April 27th 1854, the regiment took the two o'clock train arriving in Cork at 5 p.m., having come one hundred miles in three hours. On arrival we were quartered in Cork Barracks for that night. The following morning we were conveyed to the transports, which rode at anchor in Queenstown Harbour, by two small tug steamers.

This harbour is unsurpassed for capacity and safety. Its entrance is by a channel three miles long by two miles broad, defended on one side by Forts Camden and Carlisle. The upper portion extends for about five miles below the city to the passage. Within the harbour are several islands, the principal ones being Great Island, on which are situated the fortifications of Queenstown, Spike Island where stands a bomb-proof artillery barracks and a convict depot, and Rocky Island on which are situated some powder magazines. There are some fine trees on both sides of the harbour, as well as some handsome cottages and villas. The architecture of Queenstown presents some objects of interest in the way of churches, fine shops and large brick residences. The streets are wide and many of them afford a fine view of the shipping in the harbour.

It is to my mind one of the nicest places in Ireland. The right wing were all on board with the exception of some of the officers and their families. The privates of each company were shown their berths and mess tables and the ships' officers told off the women and children to their berths. The bustle incidental to getting a ship under weigh was very speedily got over and the accommodation found for all hands, gave eminent satisfaction. Rolls being called and all reported present the watches were then told off. The sailors and soldiers manned the capstan and the band got ready to play. At 3 p.m., the captain gave the order to "weigh anchor" whereupon the band struck up "Rule Britannia" all hands keeping time to the music whilst making the capstan revolve merrily.

As soon as the anchor was tripped the sails were unfurled and we moved out of the harbour amid cheers from the shore which were gaily replied to by us, and we were soon bowling along with quite a stiff breeze on the bow. The men were served out with hammocks, and each received one tin plate, one blanket, one pannikin and one meat dish, and one soup-can for each mess. At 5 o'clock the tea bugle sounded when orderly men repaired to the cook's gaily for their tea and afterwards served it out to the various messes. After tea, the men went on deck to chat and smoke. At 5.30 the rations bugle sounded, when the orderly men proceeded to draw the rations for the next day, consisting of beef and salt pork and on alternate days flour, raisins, currants, biscuits, tea, sugar, cocoa, mustard, vinegar, salt and pepper. They made the plum-pudding for dinner and tied it up ready to boil after breakfast next day.

The ship was being propelled by a strong wind right over the larboard bow and under a perfect cloud of canvass. At 6 o'clock the boatswain piped "down hammocks" which at the signal were all swung and as the last call sounded at 9 o'clock the men all crawled into them. Towards night the wind freshened considerably and the sky began to assume an angry appearance, rendering it necessary for the captain to shorten sail and otherwise make preparations for a storm. All night it blew a perfect gale, the wind still remaining in the same quarter. Before long still more canvass had to be taken off the ship, but her motion was so violent even under all but bare poles that everything moveable was dashed about like peas in a rattle. We then were going along at the rate of about 11 knots an hour.

Next morning, at 8 o'clock, we had breakfast comprising hard sea biscuit ("hard tack" as it is called), and cocoa which latter was excellent and after the meal was ended, all hands were ordered on deck with the exception of the orderly men, who prepared the meals and kept the place clean and in order. At 12 o'clock the sound of the grog bugle was heard and there were very few absentees from *this* parade. We were served out with a half gill of "rum and two waters." A few of the men suffered from sea sickness, but most of them put in an appearance at their dinner of salt beef and plum pudding. By the time dinner was over a change had taken place in the weather and we were now enjoying a bright sky and shining sun: a most agreeable sight to us landsmen. The mess gathered upon deck to smoke and talk, the progress of the ship forming a staple article of conversation.

This subject was apparently, the first thing in the morning and the last at night in everybody's mind. The sailors made themselves very agreeable and frequently enlivened us with sea songs whilst engaged in their various employments. By 6 o'clock a.m., the decks were all clean and dry, and at 9 o'clock, the doctor ordered all women and children on deck. Good weather still prevailed and everything was very pleasant, the ship travelling with close reefed canvass: shortly after sun down, the wind commenced to blow from the north-west and we were making splendid time across the Bay of Biscay, By this time the motion of the vessel had ceased to trouble any of us and many of the officers and men assembled on deck to watch our course and look out for land.

The wind had somewhat increased if anything on Sunday morning, and during the 24 hours we made upwards of 190 miles. Divine service was held on the main deck at 10 a. m., which was conducted by the captain. When service was over all hands noticed that the wind had abated considerably but the ship running before it still continued to make about the same rate of speed as she had been doing. We slept well that night and the following morning, the sailors could have been seen reeving ropes and making their preparations to put the ship snug as they said we were going to have a storm, not very pleasant news for us. The glass had been falling rapidly and we were on the look-out for squalls literally, which sure enough turned out to be correct, for before the morning was over we had it in earnest and with a fierce wind and heavy sea the ship was very soon plunging about as if it were going to the bottom every minute

The boatswain's whistle was plainly audible above the howling of the storm and the creaking of the strained spars and cordage. The sailors were ordered to take in sails and haul the ship close. One particularly heavy sea struck us nearly amidships and in a moment there was a confused mass of men, women, children, and movables knocking about in all directions. As usual there was a perfect chorus of screams from the frightened women and indeed many men did not look particularly cheerful about the matter, but in another minute we were dashing onwards once more. Fervent prayer was the order of the day, or rather night, on board for by this time it was past 12 o'clock and pitch dark. In fact all acted as though they momentarily expected to be called before their God. It was both touching and awe inspiring to find so many strong men acknowledging in the hour of peril, their utter helplessness.

The decks were constantly being completely washed by vast bodies of water and the night was a fearful one. The sky was as black as ink and seemed as if it really closed down upon the ship like a funeral pall. Most of the men, women, and children had undergone a second attack of sea-sickness. The storm continued with great violence all day Monday, and at night nobody could get anything to eat even if their fright had not taken away their appetite, on account of all the fires being put out. The hatches were battened down and nobody was allowed upon deck except the captain and sailors. At about 2 o'clock on the Tuesday morning the wind changed and blew more on our larboard quarter, finally dropping. The boatswain piped all hands to square yards and make sail and by 12 o'clock we thanked God for calm weather once more. The usual grog bugle found all hands quite ready for their share of stimulant.

At 6 in the evening the weather had become as fine as anyone could desire and, after our late frightful experience it seemed like a blessing and we felt very happy in consequence. The night also continued fine and for the first time since the beginning of the storm we all enjoyed a sound refreshing sleep. When I went on deck, there was scarcely a breath of wind. After breakfast the women and children went upstairs and then the lower decks were scrubbed and cleaned. At the summons to dinner they went to their respective quarters and in the meantime the upper deck was well washed, cleaned and once more put into something like order. I was a good deal surprised when at about 10 a. m., the following morning the lookout at the mast head cried out "Land ho!!" I could see no land and it was quite a long time before I did, for to me, what they called land, only looked like a cloud in the distance.

When we were about 10 miles off, however, its highest peaks, the lofty headland and cliffs of cape St Vincent were plainly discernible, together with its light-house and convent. It was the first land we saw. On our right we caught a good glimpse of the white mountains of Africa as we crossed Trafalgar bay. On the left, close to us as it seemed we had the coast of Spain and as the crops were then very nearly ripe the view was enchanting. Shortly we came into the straits of Gibraltar and were soon abreast of the Rock itself which of course was of great interest in the eyes of all aboard and upon sight of which the ship hoisted her flags. We cast anchor in the harbour of Gibraltar and shortly after the health officers' boat flying the yellow flag came off to us to enquire as to our sanitary condition.

As our doctor, however, gave us a clean bill of health, we were immediately given orders to disembark, May 13th 1854 at 6 p. m. The right wing formed in open columns of companies right in front of the New Mole. Considering the roughness of our passage and the knocking about we had all had, the men looked both well and clean. The band and pipers of the 92nd Highlanders and the band of the 89th played us to the Caseman Barracks, where we were quartered. We were followed by a motley crowd of Irish, English, Spaniards, Italians, Moors and Jews. We were welcomed by several soldiers from the garrison who were pleased to see a new regiment arrive to share their military duties. About half past two the following day, the *Dunbar* arrived having on board the left wing. They landed at 3 p. m., and joined head quarters shortly afterwards. No 6 company proceeded to Catalan Bay outside the city gates, on detachments.

The regiment was exempt next day from garrison duty in order for them to get their baggage and settle down in their quarters. The guards with colours were trooped every day at 10 a. m., (Sunday ex-

44

cepted) on the esplanade under the field officer, assisted by the town major just the same as if at home. All regiments going to Gibraltar are obliged to furnish so many men to the Royal Engineers, and I was one detailed, and worked with them at the New North front facing the Spanish lines also in the Government works, during the time I was at Gibraltar.

This is the strongest garrison in the world. It is situated on a narrow neck-land of Spain, which extends four miles out into the Mediterranean Sea. The Rock itself, towers about 2,500 feet above the sea level being one of the largest rock formations in the world. Algiers lies five miles south of Gibraltar. The west forms a fine harbour. It is a large seaport town called Algezier. The climate is very warm and pleasant throughout the entire year. The troops have bathing parades twice a week. At 4 o'clock in the morning when the gun tires from the rock, the city gates are opened by the town major with a posse of guards. The market now opens and the Spaniards come pouring in with a plentiful supply of water melons, grapes and all kinds of fruit which can be purchased for a mere song. Goats milk is the only kind in use in Gibraltar. On the queen's birthday, the troops in garrison consisting of two companies of sappers and miners, three batteries of Royal Artillery, and four regiments of infantry, were drawn up in line on the neutral ground at the North front.

At noon each man was furnished with 12 rounds of blank cartridge. On the stroke of 12 by the tower clock a gun was fired from the Sky Battery. This was the signal for a Royal salute. The batteries on the rock as well as the men-of-war in harbour, fired the regulation 21 guns each. The troops then fired the *feu de joie*. After the smoke had cleared away, they waved their *shakos* in the air, and gave three cheers for Her Majesty. The spectators of whom there were some thousands enjoyed this grand military spectacle in honour of the queen's birthday. The troops then marched past in slow, quick, and double time, and were then divided into armies and subsequently put through a sham fight which lasted till 4 o'clock.

We frequently had sham fights, and a general review once a week during the summer months. About the fifth of November we received orders to prepare for active service in the Crimea. Then there was the usual packing of baggage. The evening before embarkation our company was entertained at a supper by the 39th regiment of Grenadiers, whom we had often met and done duty with in the same garrison and a friendly feeling had sprung up between the officers and men of both

45

companies. The captain and officers were present and after the cloth was removed, the President proposed a toast to the "Queen" which was drunk with a good will, followed by three cheers for Her Majesty. The captain of the 39th then stood up to propose the health of their guests. He said:

> Brother officers and soldiers! In the name of the Grenadier company which I have the honour to command, allow me to extend to you, our brothers in arms, the right hand of fellowship and a hearty welcome. I think this garrison which has been so jolly is about to be broken up by the Gallant 17th Royal Bengali Tigers who are going to join the army in the Crimea. I must say that we heartily regret that it has not come to our turn to share the honours of our comrades in a brush with the Muscovites, but we hope before many days, to have the pleasure of joining you on the battlefield, there to share the glories of the British army in fighting for our Queen and country, and of leading such men as I now see before me at this hospitable board, against our common enemy the Russians. We tender you frankly the hand of military comrades and instead of firing a *feu de joie* of complements, it is the duty of those who remain behind to drink the health of those who "are proceeding on active service. A bumper then boys! and let us say, good health and God speed the Gallant Tigers.

With three times three the glasses were drained, whilst the band struck up "The British Grenadiers." Captain John Croker was then called upon to respond and said:

> Brother officers and men of the 39th regiment. This cordial reception and courtesy on your parts demands our warmest acknowledgements which I in the name of my company have the honour to convey to you on this occasion I therefore propose a health towards the Grenadier company of the 39th regiment, with whom we are about to part. Charge your glasses!

And the toast was drank with all the honours, to the appropriate music of "Auld Lang Syne" and the company song of "They are Jolly good Fellows."

After staying here for two days during which time we took on board a battery of the Royal Artillery and large quantities of ammunition we once more weighed anchor.

CHAPTER 5

The Night Before the Battle

Tomorrow, comrade, we
At the great Redan must be
There to conquer or both lie low,
The morning star is up
But there is wine still in the cup,
And we'll take another tot ere we go, boys, go,—
We'll take another tot ere we go.

Y is true in warrior's eyes
Sometimes a tear will rise
When we think of our friends left at home;
But what can wailing do?
Sure our goblets' weeping, too,
With its tears we'll chase away our own, boys, own,—
With its tears we'll chase away our own.

The morning may be bright
But this may be the last night
That we shall ever pass together here.
The next night where shall we
And our gallant comrades be,
But, no matter, grasp the sword and away, boys, away—
No matter grasp the sword and away.

Let those who brook the lot
Of the Russian great despot
Like cowards at their home they'll stay
Cheers for our Queen be given
Whilst our souls we trust to heaven,
Then for Britain and our Queen, boys, hurrah!

Hurrah! Hurrah!!!
For Britain and our Queen, boys, hurrah!

On the morning of our departure, the regiment paraded on the square of the casement barracks for the last time, and having been called to attention by Colonel McPherson, K. C. B., received the words of command "Quick march!" The men marched off through the town to the tune of "The girl I left behind me" played by the band, followed as usual by a large crowd. *En route* to the New Mole where the steamship *Tamer* was lying alongside the wharf waiting to take the different troops to the seat of war, we were heartily cheered. The parting with our relatives and friends was a sadly trying ordeal, but our queen and country required us to meet the Russians in mortal combat and we had to go. At 11 o'clock all being ready, the Captain gave the word, and the steamer moved out from the wharf, the band playing "Auld Lang Syne." As soon as the vessel rounded the New Mole, her speed increased and soon Europa Point with its barracks and batteries was turned.

Next morning the deck was washed at 5 o'clock, and at 10 a. m., the commanding officers' parade took place: the men appearing in first class condition. The weather was fine and the ship moved along at good speed. A Mediterranean sunset being somewhat of a novel sight to the majority on board, caused us to assemble on the deck to witness it and certainly we were delighted and surprised at the magnificent sight. The following morning after parade, the men amused themselves as best they could, by playing games, etc. After dinner the band played on deck, pleasing all on board with the fine martial music. For three days we had Africa on our right as we passed down the Mediterranean. By 7 o'clock a. m. in the morning of the 3rd August, land had been reported by the lookout.

As we neared the spot, it appeared to us a rocky island. It was Malta. Those who had not visited the place before, were somewhat surprised at this curious city. Batteries on all sides fairly bristled with guns. To the right of the city could be seen spires and domes above the houses. The harbour was crowded with shipping. We made a grand passage of 1300 miles in three days. Soon after our arrival a coal barge came alongside and about 60 Maltese commenced loading us with coal. They carried the coal on their backs in baskets. A great source of amusement both to officers and men, was watching the divers who came alongside in small boats. The boat was managed by a boy thus leaving the diver at liberty to attend to himself. Their dress consisted of a light pair of drawers and a loose shirt. Having ranged up just below the gunwale over which we were leaning, and taking off his upper garment, he said in broken English, "Sixpence! me dive for sixpence! me get him quick!!!"

One of the officers threw a sixpence into the water, supposing he was going to the bottom for it, but he knew a much easier way of catching it. The moment it struck the water, he was after it like lightening and rapidly diving with his hand under the coin fished it up, put it between his teeth and reappeared on the surface. He earned a good many sixpences in this way before he left our ship. After staying here for two days during which time we took on board a battery of the Royal Artillery and large quantities of ammunition we once more weighed anchor. As our steamer left the buoy, she was cheered by the populace generally as well as the soldiers in Fort St Elmo and St Anglo. Our men were by no means backward in returning the compliment. The town of Valetta with its strong forts batteries and houses, soon faded from view as the gallant *Tamar* gathered way. We had a trackless expanse around us, but in the distance we could see mount Etna to the Northwest.

We had one dash of bitterness in our cup of pleasure, by discovering that the captain in command of the detachment of Royal Artillery had committed suicide by cutting his throat in his cabin for some reason which was never discovered. The ship was then headed for Malta where we handed the remains over to the proper authorities and once more steamed out of the harbour on our voyage. A pretty stiff breeze springing up about this time enabled us to make use of our sails and sent us along merrily. By the evening of the following day we had run 240 miles; not bad going in 24 hours. Sunday, was gone through much as usual, *viz* divine service in the morning. There was a deck parade on the following day at 10 a. m., and the band played in the afternoon. Towards evening the wind rose, and although the sun went down in a clear sky there were suspicious indications of bad weather about

And very soon we had a second experience of what a gale at sea is like. We made land about daylight the following morning, having taken on board a Greek pilot. As we closed in with it villages of white houses as well as snow capped mountains became visible. About 8 a. m., we passed Cape Matayson. As we rounded the angle of the cape we met the wind right in our teeth, and the billows were white with foam. Our progress was necessarily somewhat retarded, but by 9 p. m., we had passed Milo at which time the storm had increased. About 10.30 p. m., the wind had come aft, the ship rolling very heavily at the time so much so in fact that we had to hold on to stay ropes or anything we could find to prevent being thrown about all over the place. Some of the horse stalls were broken loose and slid about the deck like, as one of the men observed, "a hog on ice," and the horses had to lie against the bulwarks.

By noon the following day, however, the weather had moderated and the sun was shining. This gave the artillery men an opportunity to put up the horse stalls and secure the horses. The Greek coast trending to the left with its rugged mountains and some good sized towns were passed. Several windmills erected on the beach were to be seen, as we swept through the Termain passage accompanied in our course by several white sailed crafts.

To the left was the Gulf of Athens, to the right the snowy heights of Mount Ida, towering nearly 5000 feet above sea level, whilst to the north the lofty Lemnos reared its head. About 4 p. m., we passed the Dardanelles Castle and here we received on board a Turkish pilot. As we passed Gallipoli about 6.30 p. m., we could see that it was a very fine city containing a lot of fine houses. From the entrance of the Dardanelles, the straits are very narrow certainly not more than a quarter of a mile in some places. We ran close to the bank in order to get sufficient water on the European side.

Opposite the town of Gallipoli, its breadth becomes greater, being about four miles. It expands to the sea of Marmora. The Turkish batteries on both sides saluted us continually as we passed and cheered us in their own way. We had Asia Minor on our right and Turkey on our left. Considering the splendid country Turkey, is it does really seem a shame to see it in the hands of such a set of good-for-nothing thieves as the Turks are. As we passed the numerous forts at nightfall we were challenged in all kinds of peculiar ways, burning blue lights which were replied to by our ship burning blue lights as well. It took us all nights to cross the sea of Marmora owing to there being a very strong current against us. Shortly after breakfast next morning, we sighted Constantinople and running passed the Golden Horn, (leaving the seven Towers and Seraglio Point behind us), we came to anchor at Constantinople amid deafening salutes and cheers, in fact we had been saluted and cheered to our hearts content every time we came near land.

Constantinople is as lovely a city as the eye could meet with, and the scenery all through the Bosphorous could only be appreciated by seeing it, as it beggars description. The view of the Marmora had particularly made an impression on all of us, the banks being studded with the Imperial Palace of the *seraglio*, and others in lines from the foot of the forts which command the entrance to the city of Constantine. The *sultan's* palace and the residences of the *pashas* are also to be found here. Altogether, we staid in Constantinople about five or six hours and then started once more for the Crimea. As we entered the Bosphorous we were struck by the beauty of the scenery and all the forts saluted and cheered the troop ship as we passed. A cold rain was falling, as we entered the Black Sea, and a heavy fog prevailed. "Black Sea weather" the sailors called it, and this continued for some hours past daybreak.

After breakfast we set to work to sharpen up our swords and bayonets so as to be ready for instant use; the sailors lending us their grindstones for this purpose. When the following morning dawned, the appearance of the weather was very threatening and as we came near land, the captain standing with his telescope and the officers with their glasses also, saw at short range a tower upon a cliff, flying the Union Jack, and not long afterwards the masts of a man-of-war marking the narrow entrance to Balaclava Harbour. Our number went up at once but failed to get any response, so we entered the small harbour through a narrow passage crowded with shipping. Running alongside the ledge of rock on the left we came to a standstill in 25 fathoms of water and made fast to iron hooks fastened in the rock for that purpose. About half past two o'clock on the next day, the regiment disembarked in heavy marching order.

Previously to this we had been served with the following articles *viz*: One tent to every 16 men, one frying pan, one camp kettle, hand-saw, axe, shovel, spade, and 2 bill hooks to each mess, and one blanket with three days' ship's provisions to each man. We marched off at the word of command, the camp equipage being distributed amongst the men of the company. Rain was pouring down in torrents and we were soon wading knee deep in mud, making our journey most tedious as we tramped on through muck, mire, and heaps of forage and stores which lay totally unprotected from the weather, all around Balaclava. The weather was so bad that we had to stop outside the town and pitch our camps on the side of Kadikoie Hill, close to the plains of Balaclava for the night and while we were so doing we got wet through.

Very little comfort was experienced by us that night, in our drenched clothes and blankets lying on the wet ground but the ammunition we always managed to keep dry. Nine o'clock the picket sentries were posted round our camp, and at reveille next morning we were quickly on the alert. Our food consisted of biscuits without water, being unable to procure any of that fluid. After marching four miles through the mud of Balaclava, we looked out for the best spot to pitch our camp and finally settled down close to a stream from which we drank our fill, it tasting quite nice after our fast, and greatly helped us to get through with our hard biscuit; a rather unpalatable article to eat entirely dry.

We then turned into our tents, which were quite brightly illuminated by the flashes of the guns from Sebastopol. Our nights repose was no great improvement upon the preceding one, neither our blankets nor clothes being much dryer, and the thundering of the guns effectually prevented any of us from getting to sleep. We endeavoured to. make a camp fire about 6 a. m., the following morning, but could not find any wood anywhere about, so had to abandon the idea and consequently our meal consisted of biscuit and water as before. At the conclusion of this anything but sumptuous fare, we struck our tents and resumed our march to the front, passing through the French camp when the soldier allies turned out and cheered us, their bands playing "God save the Queen" to which we heartily responded in the most friendly manner.

We arrived at the 4th Division to which we were ordered at about 3 p. m., pretty nearly sick and tired of mud and slush, and were shown our camp grounds on Cathcarts Hill, having the honour of being the first regiment in front of the 4th division. Before pitching tents, two thirds of the regiment were detailed for the trenches that night. The late hardships and two nights exposure to wet and cold had told upon the men and in consequence quite a number were obliged to report themselves sick, and were ordered into hospital tent. On the completion of tent pitching we were particularly anxious to get a view of Sebastopol and his surroundings, for which purpose we climbed to the top of Cathcarts Hill from whence we could see splendidly. There was the city and its batteries, also a Russian camp where the reserve army was placed.

At sunset the covering party were paraded on the brigade grounds and after dark marched for the first time to face the enemy, a field officer being in charge and each party having their officers. On our way down the Russians catching sight of us immediately opened a heavy fire but at every fusillade we lay down until the round shot, etc., had passed over us and by this manoeuvre we managed to dodge them until we relieved the party in the trenches. The enemy had found out our times for relieving and invariably opened a continuous and harassing fire upon us in the vain hopes of either driving us from our trenches or preventing the work going on. After the trenches had been taken charge of one hundred and fifty men were told off to build batteries in the second parallel and to cut advancing trenches. We were formed into gangs of twelve men, each gang being in charge of a non-commissioned officer.

Here I may as well inform the reader, that all such work as battery building, trench cutting, etc., etc., was always performed under the superintendence of the Royal Engineers. The work was very hard not to mention the danger both from shot and shell and 12 o'clock was very welcome to us bringing as it did the hour for "grog" a half-gill of rum, which however although not much, gave us fresh *spirits* both literally and figuratively to continue the work. Whilst working, a man was always placed on the lookout for the flashes of the enemies' guns and when he perceived one, he called out "Down," on which we at once lay down in the trenches. After a little while, I found that I could tell to a nicety where the shell would drop, by merely taking notice of its altitude in transit from the mortar. In the case of a shell we got behind the traverse.

The flashes from our own guns and mortars, gave us plenty of light to work by, but did not afford the enemy much advantage. They soon seemed to realize that they were wasting a greater part of their ammunition and began to send out *fire balls*, that is pierced cases containing oakum and tar which blazed like so many bonfires and played the mischief with us as they enabled the enemy to direct their lire with greater precision. We were very hungry when morning came, but only the same old fare of biscuit and cold water was obtainable. All through the night the Russian fire was not slackened, but was continually poured upon us from the Crows Nest, Garden, and Flag staff batteries.

During the day we tried several shots with the "Old Brown Bess" at about 800 yards. Oh! how we did long for a good Enfield rifle then, instead of the smooth bore with which we were armed! ! On the 18th December 1854, I was one of the covering party in the advance works, in front of No. 11 battery on the left attack. One of the shells from the Flag-staff battery exploded in the trench and a splinter of

17TH REGIMENT OF FOOT OFFICERS

it pierced my head causing a deep and serious wound. This was the first blood drawn in our regiment. Two men lifted me up, and carried me to Green Hill Battery where my hurt was attended to by a navy doctor.

As I was being conveyed there, a cannon ball fired after us by the Russians whistled past us close to our ears: barely raising us. The doctor after dressing my wound endeavoured to persuade me to go to the hospital, but I volunteered to join my comrades again and try to get revenge on the enemy. I resumed duty as soon as the doctor had finished with me, and under cover of night we marched to camp where we made our usual meal of biscuit, cold water and as a change, a little raw pork. We were soon lying down in our tents, our feet to the pole with our knapsacks under our heads and our blankets round us, without any warm food or fire. Not knowing one hour from another when we were going to be attacked, we were ordered not to undress so as to be in readiness to turn out at a moments' notice.

The reader will perceive that our surroundings could not be called luxurious, even by the greatest stretch of imagination. During the night, an alarm was given that the enemy had advanced on our trenches in great force, upon which we were turned out and marched down. As we went down to the trenches at the double, the roaring of the cannon and cracking of musketry was dreadful, our way being lighted up by the flashing of the guns. By the time we reached the Green hill trenches, the enemy had been repulsed with great loss and many of them lay dead and wounded all around the scene of action. Our loss was comparatively trifling, nine men wounded and four killed. We returned to camp and rested undisturbed until the morning feeling both tired and wet.

At 8.30 a. m., Lord Raglan and his staff came to get a good view of Sebastopol from Cathcarts Hill. He was accompanied by General Pelassier and his staff. As soon as breakfast was over, all available men after furnishing the trenches were employed in carrying round shot and shell from the siege train to the trenches. This work was very hard as each man had to carry two round shot weighing 68 lbs apiece one being slung in front and the other behind in biscuit bags, sinking in the mud at every step. This and dragging heavy guns into position occupied the whole day.

In the evening a comrade of mine and myself went over to see Michael Kelly a friend of mine from Galway, who was in the 88th regiment and who had fought at the Battle of Inkerman. He gave us a long account of that battle which for the benefit of my readers, I will relate as I heard it from him as near as my memory will permit.

Chapter 6

Kelly of the 88th's Account of Inkerman

The rattling of musketry, the roar of big guns, and the bursting of shells, such was the reveille on the 5th November 1854. The British troops rushed from their tents into the murky air outside, where the men bewildered by the fog, darkness and uproar scarcely knew where to expect the unseen enemy. All was surprise and confusion. Round shot flew past with angry rush and bursting, shell scattered ruin and destruction on all sides. Tents were knocked over and torn to ribbons. Round shot, after upsetting some poor victims bounded down to where the cavalry horses were placed. Near the windmill orderly men in camp had just begun to struggle with the rain endeavouring to light a fire for breakfast. The outlying pickets were surprised and forced to retire before a superior force, contesting however, every inch of ground as they fell back on the main body, when the assembly was at once sounded for the allied army, causing all to be immediately on the alert.

The alarm being given that the Russians were advancing, the tidings of dismay which they brought, were quickly verified, by the unceremonious whistling of shot and the explosion of shell amongst the tents. A strong murmur was heard mingling with the thunder and din of cannon and musketry. It swelled louder and louder and a moving multitude of Russians suddenly came into view crowding up dark ravines and slopes covered with brushwood. The first British regiments that formed were pushed forward with a battery, in double time to the brow of the hill, in order to check the enemy's advancing columns from the valley, and as the alarm spread through the camp, the brigades and divisions were rapidly formed and marched into position by their respective commanders.

They were at once met with a tremendous fire of shell and shot from guns, etc., which the enemy had placed in position on the heights during the darkness of the night. Lord Raglan on his arrival although, tenderly careful of other people's safety, gave no thought to his own, and sat immovable on his charger surrounded by his devoted staff on the top of a high mound in the hopes of getting a glimpse through the fog of the movements of the enemy during the fierce strife that was raging all around. The ground on all sides was ploughed up by the missiles of destruction that fell thick and fast. One shell came right amongst the staffs officers and close to where Lord Raglan was sitting on his charger.

As it exploded, it struck a horse, tearing the poor animal into pieces, and throwing the rider several paces from the spot; fortunately without much injury except tearing his cloths and setting them on fire. But a splinter of the same shell, broke General Cathcart's leg, in such a manner that it hung by a small piece of skin and flesh to the body. The poor man never moved a muscle of his face: he was lifted from his horse and laid on the ground whilst his life blood ebbed away, and in less than two hours he was dead, leaving behind him a memory which will ever be held dear to the British Army. Fast and furious grew one of the bloodiest and fiercest struggles ever witnessed, not only were desperate hand to hand encounters maintained on both sides, but the British were obliged to resist with bayonet to bayonet as the enemy charged again and again with demoniacal fury and determination.

"Captain McGregor!" exclaimed Lord Raglan to his *aide-de-camp* after looking through his field glass and pointing in the direction "Go down into "that ravine where our men are getting overpowered by reinforcements of the enemy. I see that Sir George Cathcart has fallen and the division is without a leader. Tell Sir George Brown to advance the left light division to support Goldie, and then take the command of the whole himself and carry the ravine at the point of the bayonet at all hazards."

The *aide-de-camp* having received the order saluted and dashed down the hill side tearing and bounding through the brushwood heedless of the bullets that whistled past his ears or the explosions of shells, and thundering of big guns and falling of missiles. At last he arrived at where Sir George Cathcart had fallen and made his way to Sir George Brown, to whom he delivered his message and who was already gallantly leading the remnant of his division against fearful odds. The message was no sooner delivered than the *aide-de-camp* who was about to retire, saw Sir George Brown fall from his horse. He had been struck by a bullet. It was a moment of intense peril the men were without a leader. No time was to be lost. The Russians who on this occasion evinced great bravery, and impelled forward by dense masses from behind, were pressing forward with the utmost impetuosity and threatened to entirely surrounded and annihilate the devoted little band. Captain McGregor seeing the danger, galloped forward with his sword raised above his head and turning his face towards his plucky followers, cried out at the top of his voice "Hurrah, boys for our queen and country, forward my brave fellows charge!!"

With a genuine British cheer the men sprung after him and plunged with the bayonet at the charge right into the moving mass of Russians, creating the utmost consternation in their ranks by this display of valour from a troop, that only a few minutes before they had considered as being as good as defeated. A break in the fog now favoured the commander-in-chief with a good view of this frightful contest through his glasses. "Captain Shaw "he said to another of his *aide-de-camp*, "ride over to "Sir Richard English and tell him to send two regiments of the reserve to the right attack where our gallant fellows are fighting against five times their number, I see that the enemy are trying to gain our flanks. Be as quick as you can and tell him to move at the double, but on no account to blow the men."

"Yes my lord" replied the *aide-de-camp* saluting and putting spurs to his horse was gone instantly, quite undismayed by the bullets which fell in showers around him. On receiving the message Sir Richard English at once dispatched the troops required, in charge of the senior colonel who however seemed somewhat confused by the fog and not being altogether certain of the way enquired of the *aide de-camp* in which direction they were to move?

"Follow me, colonel," was the brave answer, instantly returned, "I will lead the way."

They marched off at the double preceded by the gallant *aide-de-camp*, and rushed forward with the irresistible courage and impetuosity of men determined to do or die in the attempt. Stimulated by the love of queen, country, and of their gallant officers, who were so bravely leading them to glory, they tore their way through brushwood and thorny brambles as little heeding their torn clothing, and many scratches as they did the iron hail which was falling amongst them, but as fast as the men fell the ranks closed up and forward they charged fearless as ever. At last they arrived at the scene of slaughter, somewhat fewer in numbers than when they had started, but still undaunted. Here they found their comrades all but overpowered by the enemy, fighting like the heroes that they proved themselves to be.

Reanimated by Captain McGregors' bravery, although many men had fallen they still held their ground against the Russians. When the reinforcement, lead by Captain Shaw arrived, there arose a loud hurrah! loud enough to penetrate the din of the battle and hearty enough to send a thrill of fear through the very souls of those confounded muscovite thieves. This was followed by a gallant charge, and with terrific force the masses of the enemy, who howled with blood-thirsty cries of vengeance, were actually rolled back like a wave of water. It is perfectly useless for me to attempt by words to picture that awful hand to hand struggle. The daring deeds of valour, fidelity to their comrades and officers displayed by these courageous fellows on that occasion is beyond praise.

The Russians continued to advance time and time again with fresh men, and no sooner was one column routed than another took its place only however to share the same fate as its predecessor. No wonder that the British were now and again compelled to fall back to try and get a little breathing time, but they continued to fight and came up to the charge gallantly. Thousands came on where thousands had been before but only to fall victims to British pluck and endurance; either by bullet, or the cold deadly shot that those whom they opposed knew so well how to use. Whilst this charge was in progress, the extreme right led by their Right Royal Commander Prince George, was advancing with steady purpose, although its ranks had been fearfully thinned, and now dashed forward at the *pas-de-charge*, on a small battery which had previously been captured by the Russians, and with terrific force they hurled the captors through the embrasures and over the escarpments of the battery, giving vent to their feelings in cheers that seemed to literally paralyse the Russians with fear and horror, causing them to pause before daring to encounter such warriors. The pause however was of short duration. With desperate exertion they once more advanced, rallied by their officers, and dealt death and destruction amongst the British troops and for a time the fate of the day really seemed trembling in the balance.

The scene was one not easily forgotten by a spectator, the thin redline of the British persisting (with the bayonet) to resist and repulse all assaults made upon it. Had it broken or wavered but for one instant, who could prophesy what the result would have been? It would have been a terribly disastrous event to the British army. Fate seemed about to cast a blot upon a bright page of British history and for once chronicle a defeat. But no! With an almost super-human effort a terrible charge and a loud hurrah from the red line of heroes, the enemy was repulsed. They wavered to and fro, then broke and fled in the greatest confusion. British pluck had been too much for them even as it had been for Napoléon's "Old Guards." Whenever our supremacy (so roughly assailed) was triumphantly vindicated, the *Czar* of all the Russians gave way before the proud banner which has grown to be considered as the emblem of victory. This exhibition of gallantry and determination, met with well merited bursts of applause from all the spectators and the French advance was heralded by the flourish of their trumpets.

When the *Zouaves* headed by General Bosquet, rushed to the front with the light of battle on their features, their timely assistance to the battle stained and weary British soldiers, was hailed with the greatest enthusiasm. The French and English artillery co-operated and vied with each other in serving the guns and hurling messengers of death amongst the common foe, who were driven pell-mell towards the gates of Sebastopol. "And," concluded he, "History has inscribed upon tablets harder than marble, that very memorable battle and whenever the flag of Old England, that is justly described as having braved the battle and the breeze for one thousand years is unfurled, it reveals to the whole world, in letters of gold that terribly significant word "Inkerman!!!""

CHAPTER 7

Attacks on the Trenches

We all cried hurrah! when the story was ended and complimented him upon his narrative of the battle. It was then time for us to be getting back to our tents and after tattoo roll call we lay down to rest, keeping our arms however close by us and using our knapsacks as our pillows. We were soon fast asleep notwithstanding the continued noise of the guns as the opposing armies replied to each other. We could not have been sleeping more than about two hours, when, we were aroused and turned out by an alarm of a general assault being made on our trenches by the Russians. The whole of the divisions at once doubled down to the trenches where we were very soon engaged in conflict with the enemy. Indeed before we could get there, fighting was already in progress in the advanced earth works. A hot battle ensued which lasted two or more hours but at last the Russians were defeated and driven back with great loss. There were literally piles of dead left on the field.

Our victory however was not obtained without a struggle. When we started, we advanced by sections of companies up the ravine afterwards wheeling to the left and right by files. Fortunately the incessant firing of the big guns caused the scene of action to be as light as day and enabled us to see that had we not come up in the nick of time the Russians would have, in all probability captured the position through their force of numbers, although our men made the most obstinate resistance. We found out afterwards that the Russians somehow or other became aware that, owing to the French and English sentries being divided by the Russian cemetery making communication somewhat difficult between the two, that this presented a somewhat weak spot in the lines and this knowledge encouraged them to hazard an attack on our position.

In front of the left attack there were some trenches which ran down by the edge of the cemetery, from the harbour, which divides the town from the military barracks. They were commanded by the Russians on the one side and the British on the other. The cemetery divided the third division from the French attack. Therefore in order that the cemetery should be guarded, communication between the French and English sentries should have been imperative. Knowing this to be the case the Russians entered the cemetery and managed to pass our sentries by their being mistaken for French, as they answered the challenges and gave orders to their men in that language purposely to throw our men off their guard, who were bayoneted and the enemy were into our trenches before they were recognised, killing and wounding a great many of our men, a major of the 50th amongst the latter beside taking two officers and sixteen men prisoners.

When their treachery was detected however a deadly strife commenced, our brave men determining that if they had to die they would at least sell their lives as dearly as possible, and doing their best to keep back the hordes of the Russians who were all this time flocking into the trenches like hounds after a fox. After this struggle we returned to camp with our wounded and soon crawled into our wet tents thoroughly wearied and rested our selves until the orderly sergeant aroused us from our much needed sleep, at daybreak, to resume the day's toil of carrying shot, shell, and ammunition, and dragging big guns into position, or some equally hard work. I was one of a foraging party detailed that same morning for a foraging expedition to the valley of the Tchernaya River in search of fire wood. Taking our water kegs and bill hooks we started fully determined to get some wood if possible.

Crossing the plateau we reached Inkerman Heights, where that terribly hard contested battle had been fought. It stirred up a deep feeling of commiseration for those brave fallen comrades who had fought so bravely for victory, when we saw the numbers and size of the high mounds of earth marking their graves. But as we descended into the ravine on the other side of the Heights, we were greatly surprised to see over 150 dead Russians, stiff and stark lying at the bottom of the ravine in the dried up water course where they had been hastily buried: the earth that had covered them having been washed away, and there they lay in their torn clothes and accoutrements, all of which we reported at headquarters.

We continued our journey however until we arrived at an old

bridge where we climbed up the side of a steep hill covered up with wood but crowned at the summit by a Russian battery. Here we commenced work, and as fast as we cut stuff, we threw it down to the bottom of the ravine where it was collected by two of our men and tied into bundles. We did not take long in procuring as much as we could possibly take with us and with our bundles on our shoulders we escaped along the edge of the ravine, in order to elude the vigilance of the Russians. Fortunately for us we managed to get away unhurt although we were close under their batteries, which kept up a continual fire over our heads at our men opposite on the heights.

When we returned to camp our comrades were overjoyed at our success in obtaining fuel and our officers that we had got back with whole skins. It did not take long for the men to chop up what we had collected and to set fires going. Camp kettles filled with pork and salt beef were soon boiling and sending forth grateful odours which were snuffed in by the hungry men gathered round the cooking food. As soon as we had cooked sufficient food to satisfy our craving, we abandoned the fires for benefit of our officers who had been attracted by them and were agreeably surprised to find a goodly quantity of fuel and a consequent hope of a hot meal for once as they, like ourselves had been faring very badly lately. They thankfully accepted our places and sent their servants to prepare some food.

Cooking done, we all sat down on the ground and fell to with a will as this was the first hot meal that we had been able to get, since our disembarkation at Balaklava and it tasted extra good in consequence. When the meal came to an end, we had scarcely lit our pipes and composed ourselves for a little enjoyment, when the orderly sergeant entered the circle and read the general orders to the effect that in:

..... consequence of the other regiments being so reduced by sickness and death, we were to furnish from the 17th 400 men for trench duty, every alternate evening until further orders. In the meantime owing to the lull in the firing of the Russian batteries on our attack together with the favourable state of the ground consequent on the hard frost of the preceding night, the whole of the regiment will turn out at once and haul big guns down to some favourable spot near the Green Hill battery, in order to be able to place in position when night fell.

It gave us pleasure to learn that our brave and dear old friend Colonel McPherson, K. C. B., had been promoted to be brigadier-general in our own division and that Colonel Cole, one of the loyal Cole of Inniskillen was to take command of the regiment. Sir Edmond Lyons, would also take the command of the fleet, vice Admiral Dundas who was ordered to proceed to Constantinople for some purpose not made known to us at the time. In obedience to these orders the whole of the regiment which was then off; duty, were marched off to man the guns. There was no road, so we had to make one, and notwithstanding the frost, the work of hauling up the guns with drag ropes from the left siege train to the spot chosen, was very hard.

There is an old adage that *many hands make light work*, but it seemed in this case that the proverb was not conspicuous for the veracity usually accredited to proverbs for it did not make much difference apparently, as to how many hands were employed. People may talk of tugs-of-war hardly contested, but if one of them were to put their hands to those big guns, a tug-of-war would sink into insignificance beside the work of hauling them into position, through Crimean quagmire. Your qualities as a British soldier, as well as your strength as a man, were fully tested, when the gun carriage got stuck in a deep rut. Then the sergeant in charge would appeal to your pluck and nationality, in a manner that he knew right well would bring out whatever stuff was in you and cause the united strength of the men to be exerted, and almost super human efforts to be made to release the gun from its miry resting place.

Commands and exclamations such as these would be what would follow. "Men on the right! man the right wheel, those on the left, man the left wheel. The remainder, hang on to the ropes. There now boys are you all ready? then all together mind! one, two, three! away the goes! stick to her! Well done boys, hurrah! you shall all have an extra gill of rum when we return to camp!"

This encouraged the men and the gun went steadily along until it got into another trouble, and this was pretty frequently, causing another exhibition of pluck and perseverance to effect its release and eventually it was placed on the platform with its muzzle in the embrasure or placed in some other convenient spot, ready for mounting on the platform. But for every gun which we had been able to put into position the Russians had put four, and no wonder considering that they had so many more men to spare to put to the work.

After performing this fatiguing labour, we were marched back to camp where we had scarcely time to recruit our exhausted spirits on cold water and biscuit having no time for anything else, and the gill of rum which our worthy sergeant had managed to obtain for us from the quarter-master, before we were rendezvoused on the grand parade to be inspected by the brigade-major previously to marching down to the trenches. Our spirits were not improved by learning during the inspection that ten or twelve of our men had been oblige to report sick, lack of good food and general hardships and exposure in a strange and disagreeable climate being the cause. They were sent to the hospital tent, but three of them died next day and the others lingered on in a shocking state.

Next day I was again one of a forage party of fifteen men who were commanded by Lieutenant Williams. We went alongside of the Warnzdroff Road in search of more firewood the other having been used up some time ago. A donkey came rolling out of Sebastopol and my comrades and I followed him and I caught him by throwing my bed strap that I had with me, over his head and round his neck. Of course he started off, but I held on and he dragged me a good distance through the bush and rocks, cutting my shin badly and causing the blood to flow freely. Lieutenant Williams complimented me upon my success in capturing the donkey, and told me to bring him to the camp where an officer would buy him from me to bring forage from Balaklava. But I ultimately went to Dr. Simpson of our own regiment to whom I sold the brute for ten shillings.

The following day my comrades and I were for the trenches but before our time for meeting I went over to the French bazaar and bought four pounds of bread which cost me ten dollars, and fetched it into camp being the first soft bread we had tasted since our leaving Gibraltar and in consequence it was like a banquet to us. I wished I could catch a donkey every day and sell it for ten shillings but I was hardly as anxious to cut my shin bone again. After the usual inspection we marched off at sunset under the command of Colonel Lord Russell then colonel of the 1st battalion of the Rifle Brigade, the field officer of the night. Although we advanced on the trenches with the greatest caution the Russians, as I have stated, had managed to ascertain with accuracy the time of our relieving and as usual we were kept busy dodging their confounded death dealing missiles.

Every now and then a shell would fall amongst our men and this meant a gap in our ranks. However by our taking notice of the flashing of the guns we were pretty well enabled to judge where the shot or shell as the case might be would fall and we took care not to be in or near that place. On arrival at Green Hill battery half our number were told off as working, and the other half for a covering party. The party to which I belonged had been told off for a very dangerous duty under the command of Lieutenant Thompson, *viz*: to gather earth and fill sand bags and carry it fifty yards on our shoulders for the purpose of building a battery on the fourth parallel. We were under a desperately fierce fire the whole night, from the Russian flag-staff battery. Several times they prevented us from carrying on work. We had a good many men wounded and were not sorry when the hour of twelve had arrived when we retired for a brief season from labour, for refreshment consisting of biscuit, water, and a glass of rum: the latter was thankfully received from the hands of the colour sergeant who had been told off with four men to attend to the office of catering out this very needful reviver.

Having somewhat appeased the wants of the gnawing worm of hunger with the hard tack and aforesaid accompaniments, we had barely finished the last morsel when we were alarmed by the outlying sentries retiring into the trenches crying out: "Stand to your arms! the Russians are coming in strong force" which was soon confirmed by the appearance of a dark column moving steadily up the hill side, towards us. This news put us on the *qui vive* with a determination to give them as warm a reception as they had ever had. We had a splendid leader in Colonel Lord Russell, one of the bravest men that ever buckled on a sword.

In the meantime our artillery had opened a withering fire on the advancing mass and we made good use of our muskets as we blazed away continuously, but notwithstanding this seething fire which mowed them down like grass they continued to advance in good order, with a persistence and recklessness of life, worthy of a better cause. They poured into our trenches but as they came on we gave them the bayonet after discharging the contents of the barrels in their faces. This was one of the bloodiest encounters ever seen since the earth was cursed by war, and as the enemy again and again charged us, we got so jammed up as to be quite unable to shorten arms, and as we pulled the bayonet out of one man, we dashed the brains out of another with the butt-end and when we could not reach their heads we struck them on the shins.

Some of our men got clinched with the Russians and fists were frequently in use. The Russians must have had frightful loss when we ultimately drove them back, as 78 lay dead right in the trenches to say nothing of those who dropped outside or crawled away to die of their wounds elsewhere. That brave officer Captain King was in command and gave us the word to use the bayonet on the bodies of our antagonists and give it them strong, and we did as they very soon found to their cost. We formed up in close column and by this quick movement we were at a decided advantage and made the fray so hot for the foe, that they began to lose courage and gave back, trying to save their bacon being then the principal thought uppermost in their minds.

Once clear of the trenches they lost no time in doubling back on to their batteries, with us in full pursuit, but the said batteries being at no great distance we were unable to pursue them far, certainly not as far as we should have liked, for of course no sooner were our movements observed, than a most tremendous fire was opened upon us, and common sense dictated that it would be sheer madness to do anything but return to cover. We reckoned that the Muscovites must have lost between 400 and 500 men over that attack, and perhaps more. On getting back to the trenches, the work commenced of sorting out the wounded from the dead, Russians and British lying side by side. We assisted the doctors in doing all that could be done for those not past human skill and in placing them on stretchers, by which means they were conveyed to the hospital.

At 6 o'clock in the morning,, we were relieved and marched back to the camp, tired hungry and ragged, and in perpetual danger from the galling fire of the Russian batteries which seemed determined to give us no peace. The rain was still coming down in blinding torrents, soaking us through: before we had time to get to our sorry shelter. Even when we did arrive at our dreary tents, there was but little comfort in store for us for there was no fire and nothing to make one of, and in our wet clothes, chilled almost to the marrow, we devoured our biscuit and water with what appetite we might, after oiling and cleaning our guns. We were glad however despite our discomforts to lie down and try to snatch a few brief hours of sleep on the muddy ground, (not being allowed to take off anything though) as it was an impossibility to say at what minute we should be called up to repel another attack, and it would not do, dealing as we were with such a horde of bloodthirsty savages to be caught unprepared.

However, the enemy who by-the-bye must have been in even worse plight than ourselves and quite as thankful for some sleep let us alone. Shortly after 10 a. m., both sides hoisted flags of truce and the hostilities were suspended to allow of the burial of the dead, an operation that lasted some three hours. As the last spadeful of earth was thrown over the fallen, the flags were lowered, thus giving the signal for the resumption of the battle, which began to rage fiercely as ever, neither side forgetting the number of dead comrades to be avenged.

The next day a party of us consisting of about 20 men of whom I was one, under the command of Lieutenant Williams went on a five mile tramp into Balaklava for pork and biscuit, our stock having become pretty low. The weather can only be described as simply diabolical, the wind storming and blusterous, slushy, and the rain never ceasing to come down as if to create a second deluge. We had a frightfully hard time returning loaded with provisions as we were, and the night to make matters still more pleasant, was pitch dark, so that we were unable to pick our steps and many a rough tumble was the result.

Bad news awaited us on our arrival when Heaven knows a little cheering intelligence was badly needed. It appears that someone going into the tent of one of the captains of artillery a brave and trusty officer, discovered the poor fellow dead, he having been suffocated by the fumes of a charcoal fire which he had lit in his tent to try and get a little warmth, before he lay down to sleep. This sad occurrence which was deeply regretted by all, had one beneficial effect, as it proved a warning lesson to a good many of the officers who had been in the habit of doing the same thing and closing up their tents as tight as possible and many were astonished that a similar fatality had not occurred before.

The condition of the roads, now, from the everlasting down pour of the past few days, was such that the transport of shot and shell could only be carried on with the greatest difficulty and by surmounting almost crushing obstacles, proving the game and bottom of the British troops. The continual traffic too had not improved matters and all that could possibly be done was to get up small supplies of provisions to our camp at a time. Such a dreary waste of wet slush, and muck as was to be seen all around our camp and indeed everywhere else was enough to disheartened Wellington himself almost, and the worst of it was, that there was more probability of its getting worse than better.

In the darkness, the lines of fire in the air caused by the shells of both sides crossing and recrossing presented a magnificent, spectacle like a grand display of fireworks and will not be forgotten in a hurry by those who witnessed it. After we had partaken of what provisions we could get hold of, we were marched down to the trenches to relieve the party, then doing duty there. The enemy continued to keep up a shower of fire-balls from different points during the night which enabled them to see the working parties so that might endeavour to put a stop to their labours.

That night many a brave fellow went to work for the last time on this earth and many a home in the British Isles was overshadowed by the cloud of misery caused by the death of some near and dear relative. Crouched as I was beneath the traverse, whilst one of those dreadful missiles exploded a few paces below where I had taken post, I plainly saw that it did awful mischief as it fell amongst a party of our men who were repairing an embrasure which had been shattered to atoms by a round shot.

"What's the matter Mike?" said I to a man named Doolan who came towards me.

"Faith James" replied he, "Enough is the matter!"

"Who has been hurt Mike?" I then asked as I knew well that that brute of a shell had not exploded without at least wounding someone as it fell right in the thick of the men.

"Troth James" he answered "there's more nor one or two hurt, and that severely too. There's poor Malohny's leg broken above the knee. I'm afraid he won't live and several others more or less torn to pieces. Sure I'm going for the thieving doctor who is always absent whenever he's wanted. I suppose himself and ould Jones are together as usual under the rocks over beyant, enjoying their pipes and grog. But small blame to them for that same. Sure it's a stepmother that would blame them this could night. Well as I was saying I saw that same shell comin' on, and I cried! 'lookout!' to ould Sergeant Plant whom you know can niver look straight afore him in regards to his left eye that was always looking at his nose like a piper going to church! 'By your leave sergeant!' says I. 'but these fellows pass us in a hurry,' and says I to myself 'faith, there's many more where you came from and your not the only child: I never courted the family.'

"By the hoky there is Doctor Gains and Doctor McCallum down from Green Hills, so my legs are saved, the trouble of running after ould sawbones. Tare and ages James" continues he, "if that self same shell had tumbled into Paddy's Goose (a house kept by quite a decent man of the name of Antonia, and who gave us boys an almost unlimited credit in Gibraltar) faith, he would have to wait until we get back agin or somehere else he might have the daceny, to wait until we paid him? Divil a thing we thought of him though at the time, and may be after, including the long score he must have had agin, the boys. Many's the drink I took with him, to be sure I did and feel mighty thirsty now if any liquor was convenient, but you know it is only a mouthful I take by the same token which only makes a fellow long for more."

"Well Mike" said I handing him my canteen. "if you are so much in need of it, take a little to sooth your feelings."

He eagerly seized the proffered refreshment, but before he could have half satisfied his thirst, with the soul stirring contents, he was cut short by another shell, on mischief bent coming in our direction.

"May the divil fly away with those thieving Russians," he exclaimed handing me back the canteen. "They wont even give a fellow a chance to get a drink!"

We had scarcely time to take post under the parapet, when the shell exploded amongst our men, scattering fragments of bodies high in the air and all around.

"Double for the doctor Mike" said I "There will be no end of work for them directly."

"Be dad! you're about right there!" said Mike starting off at once, and in a few minutes he returned accompanied by Doctor MacDonald. Shortly after, four men cane along bearing poor Mulhony whose leg had been completely shattered and four or five others more or less severely wounded. They were taken to the Green Hill batteries where other doctors were in attendance to assist in the necessary operations. The reader must recollect that battlefield operations were not then conducted under an anaesthetic and various comforts for patients since in vogue by the aid of medical research, and consequently those operated upon were exposed to comparatively crude surgery. Of course the hospital tents were pitched in the securest places to be found, where the enemies' guns stood the least chance of doing them damage.

During our conversation, we were crouched under the traverses for the Russian fire hardly slackened, since the booming of their first gun. Orders had been issued to keep close under cover and strict injunctions given us not to expose ourselves unnecessarily. But one of our men in order to express his contempt of Russian gunnery and carried away by the enthusiasm of the moment, deliberately jumped upon the front of one of the trenches and pointing to his hinder-most part literally defied the enemy to strike it. This act of insubordination however cost him 25 lashes on the spot. We did not return their fire as we wished to save our ammunition as much as possible, whilst the enemy exhausted theirs in the vain hope of scaring our troops and demolishing the works.

But although of course their fire annoyed us very much and was a source of danger they could no more affect the valour and determination of the British than they could, like Joshua of old cause the sun to pause in its course. He took advantage of his foe in this way but such powers fortunately for us were not granted to this horde of Muscovite barbarians. The nightly mantle of darkness at last arrived much to our relief and kindly hid the hideous scene of destruction and slaughter, when we were relieved from the perilous position by the 21st Fusiliers, who were let in for a day of hard work, repairing embrasures, which had been knocked as one of our men observed "sky high and to smithereens" by the constant assaults upon them, during the last few hours.

Taking advantage of the darkness we marched into camp under as much shelter as we could find from the elements which still continued to torment us as much as ever. We began to wonder if there ever was a fine day in this climate, as this time the monotony of the scene was varied by a blinding snow storm. We were all covered with frozen ice and snow on reaching our tents, and any one with the slightest notion of what camp life, even under favourable circumstances, is, may imagine what kind of shelter a circular tent affords against a perfectly arctic fall of snow accompanied by a fierce gale of wind.

Famished, weary and tired to death after twelve hours hard fighting smoke-begrimed and unable to indulge in such a luxury of a bath we huddled ourselves together in the tent to try and get as warm as our mud saturated clothes and blankets would allow us to. The reader, who, perhaps, has never passed a night in the open air can little conceive what our condition was, but he or she, as the case may happen, probably recollects some time during their lives when they had got a bad wetting in a sudden storm, and knew the discomfort of wet habiliments for only a few hours. Let then multiply their feelings on the occasion by thirty or more and then they will fall far short of the realities of our situation at the time I am writing about.

It is scarcely necessary for me to repeat that we never slept without our arms by our sides and in fact seldom even undoing a buckle or a button as the Russian tactics seemed to be always to surprise us at night after harassing us all day; in fact to try and do what if they had known us better they would never have attempted, *viz*: to wear us out. The snow drifted heavily and on the windward side of our tents drifted right under the canvass and whirled around us scarcely less than if we had been sleeping in the open air. The roads were rendered so bad that supplies were all but cut off and indeed for some little time quite so. We were accordingly put upon half rations. The horses and mules carrying provisions up from Balaklava, got pounded and stuck in the snow and died where they stopped and fell. Worse still our men were dying by want, exposure, and hard work, even faster than the horses, and by all accounts received at headquarter the Turks were dying by the dozen at a time at Balaklava.

In fact, hostilities were almost at a standstill for want of fighting material, the men in the trenches being too feeble to fight or to work the big guns. We had one comfort, though, and that was that the Russians were even in a worse plight than ourselves, for our spies had reported them dying by hundreds from hunger And suffering exposure, and sickness, but being more numerous, they could afford to lose twenty men to our one. On Christmas morning 1854, our regiment supplied 600 men for the trenches. Our rations consisted of one biscuit and half a pound of raw pork. That day I was on duty at Green Hill battery. The Russians opened a terrific fire on the French on the left attack, and I heard Captain Smith giving orders to the gunners to support the French, and to silence the Russian flag-staff battery.

The 13 inch mortar was at once directed to that point, and one of her shells, falling at short range went flying through the roof and body of St-James Church and then blew up a large magazine, from the roof of which the rascals had flying a flag with an inscription on it purporting that it was a hospital, with the intent to deceive us. The explosion of this magazine and consequent exposure of their falsehood (a national trait by-the-bye) so maddened the Russians, that they opened several batteries upon our position and maintained a desperate fire upon us for the remainder of the day, until we were relieved by the first battalion of the Rifle Brigade, so that I for one have very good reason to remember the 25th. December 1854.

At sundown as usual we returned to our camp where, however, provisions having given out there were no rations miserable as they had been, to recruit our exhausted systems, except about a couple of handfuls of mouldy biscuits and neither fire nor wood to kindle one with, to roast the green coffee berries which the commissariat served out to us in place of regular coffee, properly ground. We had no clothing except our old and tattered uniforms that gave us no protection from the incessantly falling sleet and consequently our hospital was fast being filled up by many brave men forced to succumb to sickness brought on by our deplorable state and the week before Christmas and the one succeeding New-Year's day will long be remembered, by the procession of invalids continually being carried to the hospital tent, many of whom alas! never more to fire another shot.

On the 6th January, I was one of six men who proceeded to Balaklava under the command of Captain John Croker for the purpose of conveying to our camp some cooked pork which had been sent by some Leicestershire Ladies for the use of the Leicestershire regiment. The captain having borrowed a mule from the quarter master for the purpose of carrying on his back a bag of charcoal for his private use, we started on our march having to wade through about seven miles of quagmire. Arrived at our destination the captain, left us shivering on shore, whilst he went shivering himself with cold and hunger to forage after the pork, on board the steamer which lay in the harbour.

After two hours of "Red tape "ceremony which to us appeared two days he at last got the coveted meat landed. He then procured from a Maltese, at his own expense a bag of charcoal, for which however he had to pay on exorbitant figure, and having placed it on the mules back, we shouldered the bags of pork and prepared to return. Human nature however proved too much for us before we had gone far and our hunger aggravated by the delicious smell of the provender we carried caused us to send a deputation to the captain to procure permission to "break bulk" as the sailors say, and, he, good naturedly recognising the fact that we were in reality in need of sustenance and in fact, was sharp set himself, graciously acceded to our request and putting pride on one side joined us in our voracious attack upon a small portion of the viands.

This impromptu meal, put fresh life and vigour into us and gave us renewed courage to face our hard task and to help the unfortunate mule out of the mud into which it had settled down, and once more shouldering our bags with a lighter heart, we set forward upon our return journey. Sleet, snow, and rain beat in our faces to such an extent, and the ground was so heavy, that we did not put in an appearance at camp until past midnight. Of all the fatigues I had hitherto been called upon to take part in, this was the worst and most trying. The mule may have been a help to a certain point, but the bother of helping the poor beast out of the mud into which it repeatedly sank was a more trying thing than the carrying of our loads. Sometimes the brute got so deeply and firmly imbedded that our strength was barely sufficient to extricate it from the dilemma. People talk of *"being as obstinate as a mule*" but the way that mule put up with being hauled and pulled around to get it free and the patient way in which it plodded on after us every time it was released from its difficulties, has gone far to eradicate the popular unfavourable opinion of that animal in my mind.

On our arrival at the camp, our considerate captain did not only a very kind but also a very wise action by giving to each of us a glass of real Hennessy's brandy from his private stock, a case of that liquor having been sent out to him as a Christmas box, by a relative of his. in Dublin. I verily believe that this timely kindness, saved us from being laid up with some disease or other after our exposure to such a hard time as we had had. I should mention that on leaving Balaklava we noticed that the 39th regiment had disembarked and were just forming up in columns of companies, preparatory to joining the camp before Sebastopol.

We also noted with some envy that they were well provided with warm clothing against the severity of the weather and looked very clean and comfortable in their new fur caps and long boots in comparison and contrast to us who had been out so long and had not received a single fresh article of clothing, notwithstanding that, that, which we had on was in tatters, the result of the continual battles, sorties and night attacks, trench work, and other arduous duties. Even our boots were hardly any protection to our feet, the leather having shrunk from the wet and our feet having swollen from the cold. Many of the men had a hard time to get their boots on at all and in some cases if they took them off, they could not get them on again and had to go on duty bare footed, as many an old Crimean veteran can testify today. Next morning there was what in a picture, would be called a beautiful scene of exquisite whiteness which presented to our view the whole of the mountains of Balaklava, and McKenzie's heights and along the valley on the south side of the Tchernaya River covered with several feet of snow.

To us however, in our height the beauty of the scene was somewhat lost as we were not in a sufficiently comfortable frame of mind to enjoy it greatly. The cold was greatly increased by the high wind and caused the mercury in the doctors thermometer to register many degrees below zero; it seemed us if it blew sheer through our very bones and on more than one occasion my hair has actually frozen to the cape of my coat. This weather would have been far more welcome to us than the wet and mud, had we only been clad in suitable garments to resist the climate, but as our clothing was totally inadequate for the severity of a Crimean winter, our hardships not only in the trenches but at all other times may be conceived.

Fancy leaving the earth works or whatnot after twelve hours heavy fighting, only to come into a miserable wet sloppy tent, without fire or sufficient food! ! cramped and half frozen to deaths no chance to procure a hot meal or even a warm cup of anything of which we were so much in need. But even these very necessary articles were not missed so much as a pair of proper long boots to protect our feet and lower part of the legs. It is true that most of the officers had taken the precaution to provide themselves with long boots and they found them invaluable. Our mitts were so completely worn out that, not being able to go without entirely, necessity which is truly said to be the mother of invention compelled us to improvise a pair out of our blankets, which answered the purpose tolerably well.

During the hours we could get for sleep our greatest difficulty was to prevent ourselves from getting frostbitten owing to the intense cold. But one poor fellow, a good soldier, and faithful comrade, named George Martin, met his death by freezing in his tent during one bitter night. Another of our comrades, named Stevenson, was also found frozen to death in his tent one morning by the orderly corporal when rousing the men and we had several of the officers and men badly frostbitten who however escaped death, and the number admitted into the hospital from the trenches who had been nearly frozen to death amounted to over 60 in twenty-four hours. The loss of horses to the cavalry division amounted to over 70 within a few days and it was sad contemplate on the number of brave men who had been spared death from the bullets of the Russians only to meet with it in a more terrible form from hardships, and the prospect of many more falling victims in the event of this cruel weather continuing.

The commissariat horses and mules were dying by the score, and it seemed the most likely thing in the world that the men themselves would be the next to follow and that very quickly, as not a day passed without death claiming one or more as its victims from starvation and exposure. We had a great deal more fear of the weather than we had of the entire Russian Army and it was a general wish that we should be led against Sebastopol and either take it or die in the attempt, a quick death being preferable to such agony as death by inches caused by lack of even the commonest of common necessaries. Like true soldiers we did not mind death with honour, but to die like neglected dogs, went sorely against the grain.

It was a depressing sight to see day after day, comrade after comrade conveyed to the new burial ground which had been opened on the hillside, to be laid in one of the numerous graves already opened to receive an inmate, no funeral honours being paid for lack of time and men, all available men for duty being engaged either in the trenches or on ammunition fatigue, that is supplying the trenches with shot and shell as I have already described. The soldiers although bearing all without murmuring, felt their spirits getting lower and lower every day and plodded along with their burdens on their backs in solemn and significant silence, despair being plainly written on their countenance, and regardless of any object whatsoever, resigned evidently to the will of the Almighty and expecting death with an apathy born of an utter weariness of their hardships.

The duty of carrying provisions and ammunitions from Balaklava to the front was no less fatiguing and trying on the men, than fighting in the trenches. Every man carried a large bag of biscuit or pork and they marched with this load a distance of five miles. Horses and mules could never have done such hard work as they could not have kept their feet and were dying all along the way. The French and Turks suffered equally with our men and had considerably more sickness among them. One day on a foraging expedition for wood, we went into several of their tents and were much astonished to find out what a frightful condition they were in. The sick and dying men lay there in their tents, whilst our sick were cared for in the hospital. January set in still colder than the weather which we had been experiencing.

Many is the night that I have worn a blanket round me with two armholes through it and when I sat down to rest I have been glad to wrap a portion of the blanket round my feet to prevent them from getting frozen. I would have given a fortune for liberty to have crept into a good sized dog-kennel if only for an hour. The cavalry divisions were getting up sheds for their horses and many of the officers were provided with sheep skin jackets, and certainly none too soon. But the men had not received any fresh warm clothing notwithstanding the fact that a quantity had been received or at all events sent out to them. The sick in the hospital on the top of the hill were great sufferers from the cold, but such supplies as we had received, proved of immense value and saved many lives.

Anyone can imagine what the situation was like with two feet and-a-half of snow on the ground. We had almost forgotten what a fire was like made with ordinary fuel, and the only things we could find to burn were a few roots and stumps which we dug up by means of a pickaxe. We were at one time so hard up for the slightest warmth that we had to burn the boards of our knapsacks to get even enough to warm our hands. Still I can truthfully assert that although we were all longing for the day when we should make some decisive movement to Sebastopol it was the generally expressed opinion that it could have been ours at any time. We were prepared to make a mighty and fearful sacrifice but have possession of that place we intended to do and in the end we did, as I shall narrate.

Let our country feel, that her soldiers who slept in mud, eat what they could in the manner that pigs would almost have turned up their noses at, and often went without food, wet, cold, and hungry, and yet never complained or turned their backs to the foe however tired they might feel, let her feel, I say, as I have reason to believe she does, proud of every man who faced the Russians, considering that that they are deserving of all praise and the brightest laurels. Let our country know them as the descendants of that great army led by their splendid chief the Duke of Wellington, the hero of Quatre-Bras, Ligny, Salamanca, and Waterloo, the conqueror of the hitherto invincible Napoleon Buonaparte in Spain and in Portugal and in fighting against such a powerful enemy at that time we had to maintain a struggle with barbarous crafty and stubborn foes and worse than all a terrible climate more calculated to produce death than a charge of cavalry, and if they triumphed through their British pluck over the foemen she may rest assured that it was only a natural outcome of that heroic blood which we inherit from our gallant ancestors.

At the time it did seem to us that more steps should have been taken to intercept the Russian supplies, or at least to harass them more in their attempts to convey their provisions into the garrison. Loaded waggons could be seen every day wending their way down the heights coming towards the north side. These should have been cut off by a *coup-de-main* at all hazards. These provisions were transferred across the pontoon bridge on the north side into Sebastopol. After we had seized the Warandzroff Road, it was thought that no other means of approach existed save by a mountain pass between them and Simpteropal on the south side but this afterwards turned out to be a mistake.

On January 16th. it being our turn for duty, 400 men of the 17th. Regiment were detailed and marched to the trenches at the usual time *viz* sundown to relieve the 18th and 57th and resume our wonted vigilance and hard fighting. Even before we had arrived we were wet to the skin and felt chilled by a heavy thaw which had set in quite as suddenly as the frost. It is a peculiarity of this climate in winter that one cannot tell whether one is to be frozen or drowned before night the changes being so very sudden. When we arrived at the trenches we found them half full of water and mud: a pleasant prospect for us to have to pass the night up our thighs almost in ice cold water.

We had no sooner relieved our comrades than it became evident to us that the Russians were very actively engaged, evidently celebrating one of their great festivals of which their church has many, for, flaming bright lights shone from the windows of all the private houses and public buildings. They also lit watch fires and bonfires on the north side of the harbour and illuminated the heights over the Tchernaya River with rows of lights in the form of a cross, which shone brightly through the darkness of the cold wet winter night. Our sharpshooters however lay down right in front of our advanced earth works with their muskets loaded and capped ready to fire at our enemy whenever he showed his head, body or indeed any part of himself and keeping a watchful eye on every embrasure in front of us so that the enemy could not make a movement that was not instantly noticed by our men and at once either answered or guarded against.

About the hour of twelve all the church bells in the city began to peal and clang and it was then evident that the Russians were engaged in performing some solemn religious ceremony amid the glare of torches and the pomp of gorgeous ritual, and with chant and hymn heard only by the demon of war. The Greek priests were exciting to frenzy by their gesticulations curses, prayers, denunciations, and in fact by every means in their power, the Russian soldiery. They harangued them in the most passionate language, and by the most powerful appeals they knew how to apply to stir them up to sally forth like the semi-savages that they were under vain promises and prophesies that they were certain of victory against the British who were represented to them as being nearly half starved weakened and an easy prey to conquer and their superstitions zeal was ardently appealed to, to drive us, the *infidels* and heretics from before the impregnable walls of their city.

Thus the priests worked upon their people and stirred them up to do the best that their natures would let them. Notwithstanding that they were apparently engrossed with their religious ceremonies, we were warned not to relax our vigilance in the slightest. On the contrary, all our advanced posts were strengthened in order to be in readiness for an attack on our position which we fully expected to be the end of their church business. And it was as well that we were prepared, for soon after the Russians emerged from their various places of worship, which was about one o'clock in the morning, they gave three united patriotic cheers which were born on the breeze to the ears of our artillery and blue Jackets, who at once responded by opening a vigorous fire upon them seconded by the French on our flanks.

The Russians, not to be behindhand, opened on us one of the fiercest cannonades we had up to that time experienced. It seemed as if the flame and smoke from their batteries poured forth not in jets, but one continued blinding flood. The city was as much illuminated by the flashes of guns and mortars, and the bursting of shells as though every house had suddenly turned on an immense electric light, so that we could see the houses, buildings, etc., as well as the batteries as distinctly as in broad day light. The latter seemed fairly swarming with soldiers and before the sound of a musketry volley had died away, the roar of the big guns and the hurtling of shot and shell filled up the space to be again followed by another heavy volley from the small arms. Cannon balls passed over our trenches rapidly like a flight of starlings, ploughing up the ground into furrows wherever they fell or struck our parapet with an ominous thud.

Our gunners were obliged to seek shelter, close under cover of their batteries, and could barely reply to the continued volleys. Sometimes a round shot would tear up the parapet, knocking, sand bags, gabions and fascines about the men's heads, not unfrequently knocking the men's heads off. Nevertheless our superior gunnery was very manifest and our missiles of destruction were sent into the enemy's embrasures with such terribly correct calculation that many of their batteries were dismantled and their guns silenced. Our gallant artillery, ably seconded by the Blue Jackets, gave so good an account of themselves, that they effectually prevented both the Garden and Crow's nest batteries from doing any more mischief. As these two batteries had been playing very heavily on our left attack it was a great point gained to have them put *hors de combat*.

Whilst all this fighting was going on, a strong body of the enemy, under cover of their batteries had been pushed up the hill sides on our advanced works over the Worandzroff Road. The alarm was given at once, by the outside sentries and we lost no time in mounting the parapet. As soon as they came close enough to make our fire effective we gave them a withering volley from right and left, and the field

80

officer in charge at once dispatched messengers to the other parallels for reinforcements, which arrived in good time to assist us in driving the Russians from our trenches. Notwithstanding our warm reception of them, the enemy persistently and rapidly advanced on our works, although we blazed away at them as fast as we could load and pull trigger. When they came to close quarters we stood on the escarpment of the parapet and gave them the bayonet left and right in fine style. Our officers fought in the bravest manner and inspired the men by their example as they cut down foe after foe with every stroke of their swords.

One officer, Lieutenant Williams, in severing the thick skull of a hard-headed Muscovite, broke his sword off close to the guard. This accident nearly cost him his life, for a powerfully built Russ, seeing him disarmed made a malicious thrust at him with his bayonet, but luckily one of our men anticipating him, guarded it off and by a quick turn of his wrist drove his own bayonet through the softest part of the ruffian's anatomy, thereby saving the noble officer from being placed *hors de combat* or killed. This narrow escape from death so stimulated the officer with almost superhuman prowess, that he quickly, picked up a musket, which he clubbed and floored every Russian within wheeling distance with this novel weapon. I can assure you reader that we all fought as becometh British soldiers although the odds against us were at least ten to one, but when did British troops ever care about odds?

When the enemy found out what regular Salamanders they had to contend with and saw their comrades falling in such numbers, they began to scramble off, one or two at a time, but seeing reinforcements advancing to our assistance, they concluded that they had had about enough of it and "stood not on the order of their going," but literally ran away as fast as their legs could carry their cowardly carcasses, towards their outworks closely pursued by us up to their very batteries. Engaging with them again in the graveyard, where we had a very hard fight amongst the grave, we closed around and dislodged them from behind the tombstones, where they had sought refuge, cutting off three of their party whom we marched back as prisoners, and picking up all the wounded that lay upon the field and in our trenches. In this affair, two of our officers and eighteen men were wounded and six men killed whilst the Russians had as nearly as could be ascertained about 90 killed and wounded.

The French had also to resist a strong sortie at the same time and succeeded in driving the enemy from their works with great loss. In the pursuit, they got inside the Russian advanced batteries where a desperate hand to hand battle ensued, but by a display of great valour they managed to cut their way clear of the enemy, returning flushed with victory to their own trenches. The old saying *"after a storm comes a calm"* was realized in truth on this occasion, for next morning everything was quiet enough, except perhaps an odd shot or two exchanged as a reminder.

We were relieved that morning by the 21st Fusiliers and marched back to camp looking like scarecrows in our ragged and battle stained uniforms, tired, cold and hungry, after our hard fight and only fit to lay down and sleep for a week. What with the mud wet and muck of all sorts with which our clothing (such as it was) was saturated I don't know but what it was more of a nuisance to us than a comfort. It had thawed during the night and then turned to a sharp frost and in consequence we were ornamented at all points with long icicles which kept up a sort of rattling noise as we marched along. In the morning when we woke we found the door of our tent blocked up with snow which had fallen since we came to camp, to the depth of three and four feet in some places. Having been detailed for fatigue duty the previous night we hastened to join our party who were going to the commissariat depot for provisions.

On our arrival there we noticed that preparations were going forward for a general bombardment, very rapidly, for upwards of 80 siege guns and thirteen mortars were all ready up at the *depôt*, and if the frost and snow continued, would shortly be in position in the batteries. But although the frost made it easier to haul heavy ordnance into position, there were plenty bad effects from it in the way of men being frozen to death in the tents or badly frost bitten not to mention those who had suffered internally from its effects. When a path had once been broken through the snow the horses could get along much easier than when they had to wade knee deep in mud, with the gun sticking fast every fifty yards or so. Still the temperature was very trying, especially as we had no wood with which to build a fire. Many regiments had been served out with fur coats and long boots, mitts, guernseys, socks, flannels and waistbands, but none of these comforts had reached any of the 17th regiment except those in hospital who had received a few articles of warm clothing.

Our army presented a miserable appearance, scarcely a regiment being recognizable except by its well known camp grounds. The officers could not have been distinguished from the privates unless they wore their swords, and it was hard to see them, brought, up in the lap of luxury (as the majority of them had been) working the same as privates who had always been accustomed to rough treatment.

CHAPTER 8

Bayonets & Cossacks

On the next day 400 men were detailed for carrying shot and shell from the depot to the trenches. Having been first inspected by the officer in charge of the party, we marched off wading knee-deep through the snow which had fallen during the night, to the siege-train and from thence to Green Hill Battery. The wind blew so bitterly cold that the horses and mules refused to face it, although the men went plodding along in a dreary string through the deep snow very willingly. The aspect of these long lines of men, hardly clothed, moving slowly across the expanse of dazzling white snow, was something dismal to behold. Each man carried two round shot in canvass bags, weighing 68 lbs each, one slung before and the other behind. On completion of our arduous duties, and return to camp, we must have resembled beef that had been kept in an ice house, for we were cold through and I am sure must have looked quite as cold as we felt.

Under the circumstances, and considering the slight amount of clothing with which we had up to the present been invested the reader may be able to form an idea of what our delight was when we heard the welcome news, that the quartermaster had received amongst other useful necessaries for the regiment a good supply of long boots, sheepskin jackets, warm inside clothing, fur caps, and last, but not least, Enfield rifles to supersede the "Old Brown Bess." Much as we were in need of these essentials, conveyance of them to our camp from Balaklava entailed on our men the work of commissariat mules. However as they were all for our own especial comfort and benefit, we marched bravely, not forgetting to call in on our return at "Mother Siego's" a sort of halfway house from Balaklava, where we all had a glass of rum each or cognac brandy according to taste which considerably elevated our spirits and enabled us to continue one journey blithely, notwithstanding our burdens.

As we advanced towards the front with our loads on our backs, like beasts of burden, we passed on the way a large cavalcade of dying soldiers who were being sent down to Balaklava Hospital on horses and mules. It was a most melancholy and woeful looking procession. Many of these poor men were already in the throes of death and could not survive sufficiently to reach their destination. The mode of procedure was for two men to be carried on one mule or horse in panniers slung one at each side of the beast. The only remark made by our men on seeing a dead man pass, was, "There goes another poor fellow out of pain and suffering at any rate."

The snow having been will packed and the road made hard, we made rapid progress and arrived in camp before nightfall. The number of dead horses and mules that we saw along the way presented a strange spectacle. Some had dropped dead from sheer exhaustion and were frozen stiff', but most of them had been slain by the French and Turks who used the hides to cover their tents. The following morning, we gave in the "Old Brown Bess" and received in exchange the Enfield Rifle. We also received a goodly supply of warm clothing, long boots far caps sheepskin-coats and comfortable undergarments with a few watch coats for the sentries. The following evening the covering party for the advanced trenches was furnished by our own regiment. These were within one hundred and fifty yards of the Creek battery.

The night although clear and dry was intensely cold but we were all in excellent spirits comparatively comfortable in our new clothing. Scarcely had we taken up our position in the trenches when the enemy opened a sharp fire of musketry on us, as if they knew that we had been supplied with new arms and were challenging us to show what we could do with them. Whether or no, we were not long responding to the challenge and in such a fashion as to astonish them. Still the Garden, Crow's Nest, Creek and Barrack batteries kept up a steady fire on us during the night. Confusion could be heard within their batteries as well as their supports advancing to reinforce, and soon after they replied to our fire with a vengeance. It seemed as if their onslaught was particularly directed against our attack the whole night long.

At break of day there was fierce firing on both sides all along the lines. The Russians could not have had less than four thousand men or even more whilst we had only 1500, still the firing of both big guns and small arms was so continuous that it kept the place lighted as if with gas or electricity at the same time the lines were marked by thick curling smoke as it came out of the cannon's mouth. About one o'clock the fire rather slackened on both sides, but severe rifle shooting from behind the parapet was kept up as on every other night.

We pushed our advanced works to within one hundred and fifty yards of the Russian's batteries and on the left attack almost into the town and its suburbs, the ruined houses of which were turned into defences for their sharp shooters, and the town was consequently one formidable stronghold, from the gates to the ridge over the bay, on which the South side of the town is situated. In the night, four Russo-Polish deserters came over to us. They gave a most frightful account of the sufferings of the Russians from cold, hunger and exposure, since we knocked down their barricades by our heavy shot. They showed us as a specimen of their food, some hard black bread which they had brought with them in their haversacks, so that it was quite evident that the Russians were in as bad if not worse situation than we were and suffering quite as much hardship, notwithstanding the reports that we had heard of large quantities of food being thrown into their stores, together with other stores, supposed to have come from Odessa recently.

As soon as we returned to camp in the morning we had a good supply of hot coffee and fried biscuit, quite a luxury, nevertheless, the clear frosty weather, the transport of provisions and other munitions of war entailed considerable hardships on our weary soldiers, and worse than all, our sick in the hospital made but little progress, towards recovery, and the number who were sent down to Balaklava for treatment proved the unsatisfactory condition of our army. Those regiments which had been the worst cut up and lost the greatest number of men from sickness, etc., had their clothing conveyed from Balaklava by Spanish mules. On February 18th we had properly roasted coffee given us for the first time. This was indeed a treat compared to the manner in which it had formerly been served out to us. Vegetables however although badly needed, also, shovels, picks and spades, likewise bill-hooks were very scarce, although the latter were equally required for the purposes of clearing the camp, digging graves and chopping wood when we found any to chop.

On February the 24th as we trudged along through the deep snow to the trenches, faced by a strong piercing cold wind blowing off the Black Sea, the air was so surcharged with a thick snow blowing directly into our faces and nearly taking away our breath, that it almost rendered us blind and but for the continual flashings of the guns in the direction we wished to go, we must have lost our way. Many of the men who had suffered all the horrors of the Crimean winter for the last three or four months were so exhausted by this kind of thing that they could not keep up with their stronger comrades and were forced to drop behind.

One poor young fellow who had recently been discharged from the hospital, fell down completely exhausted. Captain John Croker, a kind and good man, at once halted the party in order to ascertain what was the matter, when to his surprise, he discovered that the man was apparently dying! But as the party were already behind time on account of the awful storm, he could not wait, but wrapping his martial cloak around the poor fellow, he tried to speak a few words of good cheer to him and told him he would at once order the guard to come to fetch him with a stretcher and have him conveyed to hospital where doubtless he would soon recover. After the party in the trenches had been relieved, our captain instructed a party to go in search of the dying man they had left by the way, as they returned to camp. When this search party headed by the doctor (who was himself a brave soldier) had reached the spot indicated, they could not for a little while discover sight or sign of him.

They called out the poor man's name several times, but got no answer, and the snow drifts were so deep that they began to despair of even finding his body. But at last they espied a peculiarly shaped growing body of snow and the doctor whose eye was the quickest of the party, at once set them to work to find out if their missing comrade was not beneath it, as sure enough he was, but badly frost bitten in one of his feet which subsequently had to be amputated. By dint of a plentiful rubbing with snow and on account of the care that was subsequently bestowed upon him, he recovered, but had lost his foot. Had we been, but five minutes later it is most probable that the poor fellow would have gone past all human skill and surgery. The fearful storm which had been raging in all its fury during the night somewhat abated during the early hours of morning having exhausted its violence, and the sun shone forth in its full splendour from a clear but frosty blue sky.

Notwithstanding the apparent fineness of the weather however, the cold still continued to be something frightfully intense, but fortunately for us our warm clothing having as I said arrived, mitigated to a certain extent its severity so far as we were concerned. There is no doubt but that had it not been for the timely arrival of these supplies, the list of dead would have been swelled to a much greater bulk than it was. People living by cheerful fire-sides and with plenty of food, can form but little estimate of the hardships, privations, and sufferings gone through by us soldiers in the Crimea when we fought for "England, Home and beauty" our queen and country. As it was, before the supplies reached us, many a brave comrade had fallen a victim not only to the Russian bullet but to a death far worse, *viz*: starvation, cold, and want of proper clothing, as it was no uncommon thing for a man to go on guard or to the trenches, clad in a manner that would make nine out of ten men shudder to appear in, even in a mild spring day in England, and this in an almost arctic climate.

All honour say I, to the British Army, that faced such fearful odds not only in the shape of human foes which we were pretty certain to conquer, but the awful and un-fightable foes of cold, wet, and fog. The atmosphere was without a cloud to cast the slightest shadow on the bright and glittering snow, and consequently we had a splendid view of the city of Sebastopol and its surroundings, despite the dazzling effects of the sun on the white surface of ice.

The pontoon bridge erected by the Russians which crossed the harbour from the Government Buildings was we could see, crowded with sailors and soldiers, who were busily employed in passing supplies to the other side, thus showing us plainly that their commissariat *depôt* lay in rear of the Redan and opposite, the fire of our batteries. Further on, towards Inkerman, the barracks and white houses, loomed up in the distance and the bells of the numerous churches were continually chiming, clearly heard by us through the frosty air. The lofty houses which occupied the hillside gave old Sebastopol a very grand appearance. Nobody was to be seen in the streets except the long coated soldiers running across the open space from one battery to the other, as they relieved guard or posted sentries.

The town was surrounded by formidable earthworks ten feet high with embrasures from which the cannons protruded in our direction. Many of the houses and cottages in the suburbs which had been rendered useless by our gunnery, as habitations, were utilized by the Russians as covers for their sharpshooters. During the day they did all they could to annoy us, by shelling our position from a mortar battery, with the result that they dismounted some of our guns destroying the platforms and portions of the earthworks. This battery was situated towards the sea, and every minute or so a shell could be seen coming towards us, across a hill that intervened between us and them, to the great disturbance of our working party who were throwing up earth works towards the Quarantine Fort.

They kept us busy looking out for these very ugly visitors. First we saw the white smoke rush into the air and form into rings, then followed a heavy dull report then the shrill whistle of the shell as it made its rapid transit through the air.. At night the approach of a shell resembled the flight of a comet, as a ball of lire having a fiery long tail passed on its way. Sometimes when it struck the earth it would sink deeply into it and as it exploded would send showers of stones, earth, etc., flying about and causing destruction to everything in its vicinity. When the smoke cleared away, perhaps the men were gathered round some poor fellow who had been struck and who was subsequently born away on a stretcher, a small mound of earth finally marking the last earthly resting place of one more brave soldier who had perhaps left a wife and little ones, to mourn his loss. Perhaps by good luck we saw a shell fly over us or out of our position and only cause a disturbance to the earth, but our reflections whilst it was on its way to us were not of the pleasantest description and the shrill whistle which heralded its approach caused many an anxious glance to be directed towards it to ascertain where it was going to strike so that we might get into a secure place under cover behind the traverse.

I was often put on the lookout for the shells, and as I have before mentioned from long practice I could judge with accuracy where it would strike and so give notice to the men of the safest retreat. After the explosion was over, we resumed our posts and our gunners paid them back in their own coin, by sending a thirteen inch shell slap into the very battery, that had just made us a present of one, and we went for them with the musket whenever they appeared at an embrasure to load or fire a gun or otherwise presented themselves. Not a man of them dare venture his head above the parapet for fear he should get a bullet through it as most likely they would, for our fellows were on the alert for a chance shot, and many were the allurements thrown out to draw them from our cover. The dodge of putting a cap on the top of a ramrod though as old as the hills, nevertheless seldom failed to "fool them" as we called it, and a shot at it was the result, when we at once let it drop and the Russians thinking it was another man down would cheer like mad and in their enthusiasm probably expose themselves thus giving our fellows who were on the *qui vive* the chance of shooting them down.

We passed the night thus until relieved at the usual time by the

1st Royal Regiment, marching back to our cheerless camp, under the accustomed shower of bullets, a compliment, the enemy never by any means forgot to pay us, but one with which we could have readily dispensed, as more than one man fell killed or wounded under their hot fire. One night it was the turn of the French to be surprised by a sudden attack, but they proved themselves equal to the occasion, as usual, gallantly repulsing the foe with tolerably heavy loss.

The following day a request was made to Lord Raglan by the Russian general Ostensacken, for an armistice to allow them to bury their dead which was granted not a shot being fired from 12 to 1 p.m. No sooner were the white flags run up on both sides than a large body of men issued from the Redan, Flagstaff, and Malakoff batteries and proceeded to carry off the dead, our men assisted by the French emerging from the, batteries on our side to perform the same errand. A few Russian officers advanced a portion of the way towards our batteries where they were met by some English and French officers when such a bowing and scraping and interchange of extreme courtesies was gone through that any one might have supposed that they were all bosom friends instead of foes.

About 1 p. m., the unpleasant task of burying the dead having been finished, both sides retired to their entrenchments the white flags were lowered and on the instant the war was raging as fiercely as ever. Once more the air became charged with every kind of destructive thing known in warfare. Meanwhile the preparations for a general bombardment of Sebastopol were making rapid progress and arrangements were being made to send up two thousand rounds of ammunition per day from the harbour to the front. Somewhere about 300 mules were pressed into the service in addition to the railway which was making rapid strides towards completion. The Highland brigade, besides all the artillery horses were employed daily in transporting shot, shell, etc., to the front. This duty came rather hard on the Highlanders after all their heavy fighting and distressed and disabled some of them greatly.

The Guards were also down at Balaklava employed at the same work. Many of them were in bad health from what they had gone through, but some of the old campaigners did not seem a bit the worse for if, they were too used to tough times to be influenced by any amount of hardship. The last day or two had been tolerably silent and calm, but it seemed the more ominous of the coming struggle which was daily expected, for the possession of Sebastopol. As we were too busy to harass the Russians they were silent although it was manifest they were hard at work strengthening their defences. Nearly the whole of our forces were employed in gathering in the necessary supplies for opening the contemplated bombardment.

By this time, we were beginning to feel the benefit of the railway as a means of transport of the munitions of war, and it enabled us to form a small *depôt* about four miles from Balaklava, which however proved too small to meet the demands made upon it, and was no sooner filled than it was emptied again, by our parties who carried the ammunition to the camp *depôt* some five miles further on. Every means were employed to push on the work of constructing the railway. Not only were the navies kept busy, but a part of the naval brigade were also engaged, to get through with the work with the utmost dispatch.

On March 5th it fell to our turn to furnish a covering party in the advance trenches. It was a clear enough night but the wind was very piercing and the enemy took advantage of the clear brightness to» treat us to a constant fire of musketry. Between four and five o'clock in the morning the din of battle was at its height and the noise was something dreadful. It was bad enough to make one believe that the end of the world had come. Under cover of a most scathing and terribly close fire, the Russians made a determined attack upon our trenches, but fortunately for us we had all along been on the lookout for something of this sort and having by some means got wind of their point of attack we had not only doubled our forces but had placed several obstacles in their way which threw them into the utmost confusion and then we blazed away at them from our trenches as they advanced.

As they jumped into our earth works or into the trenches themselves we gave them the bayonet with such hearty good will, that as usual the *Czar's* troops were forced once more to pay tribute to indomitable courage, as displayed by the, British, and took to their heels, running for their lives to the shelter of their own parapets followed by shower after shower of musket balls which we sent rattling after them, many of them being knocked over in their headlong flight for safety. Next morning the ground was strewn with the fallen, in every direction. March the 6th proving a perfect spring day, we determined to celebrate it by holding a "spring meet" and having races, which came off on a level plain near the Tchernaya River.

The Cossacks watched the proceedings, with much interest, but evidently misunderstood their nature, regarding the. whole thing as military movements of some sort and galloped about in a great state of excitement. During the races, ten of the enemy including an officer who had been degraded, gave themselves up as deserters. They were Poles, but spoke the French language fluently, and appeared to feel happy in having escaped from Russian bondage. They said:

"Send us where you please, so long as we never set eyes on Russia again." They said that they had deceived their comrades by making them believe that our sentry was one of their own outposts, and this statement was credited until the sentry fired upon them when the others discovered their mistake and precipitately fled. As the Poles were well mounted they dashed towards our line although the Cossacks tried to stop them. They made a request for the horses to be returned to the Russian lines as they were not their property, and accordingly they were taken to the brow of the hill, and set at liberty when they immediately dashed off at a great pace in the enemy's direction. We did not however allow this little incident to interfere with our day's sport, but continued the races amid all the excitement usually attendant upon that pursuit, until nearly 6 o'clock p.m.

That same evening myself and some 60 other men were detailed under the command of Lieutenant Travers, to proceed to Balaklava at 7 a. m., the following morning for the purpose of currying up to camp a supply of provisions which had been landed off a ship for our regiment. On our way down, we noted with much satisfaction the progress made in the construction of the railway. There were about three miles of it quite finished. It winds its way from the post-office in Balaklava towards Kadikoi, passing "Old Mother-Seacole's" known as the halfway house, and was; graded up as far as the 4th Division. The sleepers were on the ground along the line and a stationary engine had been placed on the hill side near Mother Seacole's, which pulled the trucks up from Balaklava.

The Turks who had never before seen a railway or even a steam engine were greatly surprised by the puffs of steam issuing from its iron lungs, together with the shrieks and screams as it was put into motion. Beyond the valley of Balaklava we had a good view of the Cossacks as they threw out their pickets and sentries all along the north side of the Tchernaya River. These sentries could see everything that went- on in the plain, from the entrance to Balaklava to the edge of the hill on which our right rested. Not a man or beast could move in or out of the town without being seen by those sentries. They had a full view of the men working with all their might on the railway and their very souls must have been filled with dire forebodings as to what it could all mean. They could see besides, the gradual rising of the white wooden huts on the hill-side and in the valleys: line after line of these extending from the cavalry camp to the heights of Balaklava.

All this puzzled them exceedingly, but it was nothing as compared to their unlimited astonishment on beholding railway trucks rushing around the hill and down the incline at the rate of twenty miles an hour. Their excitement was so great that they galloped up to the top of the hill to view them and then rode about shaking their lances as the trucks disappeared from their view. On advancing a little further we came up with Lord Raglan and his staff, who where inspecting the railway on his way down to Balaklava where he afterwards watched the progress and condition of the various military and naval departments, and then went on board the *Ariadne* man-of-war lying in the harbour, to visit some sick soldiers who were about to be conveyed to the hospital at Scutari.

It was rather a depressing sight to us, to witness what a quantity of sickness existed amongst the troops but after all it was no great wonder considering what the army had gone through, living as we had done on salt pork and beef, hard biscuit, no vegetables and very little water. We had to go down to a narrow stream to wash our clothes and frequently had to wait two or three hours for our turn.

CHAPTER 9

The French in Action

On 18th a fierce struggle took place between the French and the Russians for the possession of the rifle-pits. These pits were situated in front of the Mamelon on the right attack, and the Russian sharp-shooters used to occupy them every night, and keep up a galling fire against the most exposed part of our trenches, as well as those of the French. We supported our allies from Peels' battery which directed its fire principally against the Malakoff the latter having been playing heavily against the French during the first part of the fray. The shot from our batteries made the rifle-pits too hot a place for comfort and compelled them to quit rapidly, but at night the Muscovites crawled back again and once more resumed possession supported by large bodies of infantry.

In these encounters the slaughter of the enemy was very great, but unfortunately the French loss was not trifling either. A large quantity of ammunition was expended on both sides on account of these rifle-pits, but the French with the greatest gallantry determined to wrest them from the Russians, cost what it might, for they were a great source of annoyance. They sent a strong force consisting of about six thousand men, down close to our second and eighth division. Before dusk that evening, they were sent to the advanced trenches on our right, and the covering party and riflemen were ordered out to occupy the rifle-pits.

They advanced but found the Russians already in possession. A fierce battle then ensued, but the enemy was discovered to be in much larger force that had been expected. The French therefore could not drive them from their position notwithstanding their repeated attempts to do so. The combat was carried on by musketry and the volleys which rang out incessantly for five hours, roused the whole camp. From the constant roll of musketry together with the flashes like lightening in front, any one would have imagined that a general engagement between two large armies was going on. A notable feature of this battle was the absence of shot and shell.

About 8 o'clock p. m., the light division was turned out and took up a position near Peel's battery to support the French, under the command of General Brown. The second and third division were also turned out and marched to Green Hill battery as we expected a general sortie. By this time the French had been reinforced by General MacMahon. The *Zouaves* bore the heaviest part of this battle by far, and we could hear their officers, between the volleys, cheering and encouraging the men always succeeding in making them fight fiercer than ever. As soon as the reinforcements arrived, the French made a most determined effort and succeeded in driving the Russians out of their pits when they immediately took possession of them themselves.

The Russians, who certainly were very brave, having obtained reinforcements, again dashed at the French who however stood fast never flinching, and successfully repelling them every time. At day break after the French had gained possession of the pits, they reversed the sand-bags and loop-holes and directed a heavy fire against the Mamelon and Malakoff. The Russians were terribly disconcerted by this acquisition of the French and no doubt felt nettled at their own loss, but they had to taste the cup of humiliation, and pride's downfall.

On St Patrick's day many of the officers and men went out to look for something green to wear in their caps, etc., as a substitute for the shamrock that symbol of "Old Erin," but finding nothing green except a species of palm tree they cut pieces of that and wore them as an emblem. In the afternoon we had horse races to celebrate the day and to prove that although far from his native land an Irishman never forgets it, nor the forms and ceremonies in vogue on that day.

There was much hilarity among the crowd of sportsmen who took part in the racing and all were in good spirits notwithstanding what they had suffered, but the thunder of the big guns before Sebastopol and the explosions of shells had a slightly chilling effect. Still after the anxiety, manifested during the passage of a shot or shell, had passed over, the excited crowed cheered and shrieked as lustily as before when an infantry bob tail, took the pole from a cavalry charger, and came in first by a short head. But the effects of military influence were not wanting, for between the intervals of excitement the bands of the Irish regiments throughout the camp enlivened the day with the crash of martial music and popular airs, which sounded very sweetly in the distance.

Next night but one, our regiment furnished a working party of one hundred men at the trenches. We were told off, in gangs of ten men each to cut a new advance trench. Every file of men got a pick axe and shovel and were placed at six paces apart on the open ground without any shelter or cover whatever, and exposed to the fire of the Russians which was levelled incessantly at us in order to frustrate our attempts at trench making and throwing up of earth works. Of course we kept the usual lookout whilst all hands worked hard digging a hole and throwing up cover for ourselves. About half-past twelve, the sentries in front of us seeing a column of Russians emerge from their batteries, gave the alarm by firing upon them, but the alarm unfortunately was rather late in coming and the foe was amongst us bayoneting our men almost before we knew they were coming and we were not half prepared to meet them, in consequence.

Taken at a great disadvantage and contending against a greatly superior force, we were fairly cornered, but when a man is in a fix like this, he generally does his best to get out of it as best he can, and so it was with us, for we met them hand to hand and fought like so many lions never flinching nor giving an inch of ground with the result that we made them turn tail at last and run for their batteries as if Old Harry was after them, pursued by our shot until they got under cover. The attack was general along the whole line.

At 2 p. m., our batteries in conjunction with the French began to shell the town in return for their attack upon us, pouring our rockets and shells in successive streams, like lightening into the very heart of the city setting many of their finest buildings on fire. When next the Russians advanced on our trenches they found us well prepared to receive them as they soon knew to their cost but the French were somewhat taken by surprise, so our troops extended along a portion of their trenches overlapping them and then backing them up. On the left attack the enemy advanced in great force, and finding a somewhat weak spot in the third parallel, they killed and wounded quite a number of our men and had actually advanced to the second parallel when our covering party charged down upon them with the bayonet and drove them back after a most bloody contest.

On the right attack in front of Captain Peel's battery, the 34th regiment had a strong force to contend with and as Colonel Williams their commanding officer was leading them on against the enemy in the most gallant manner, he was severely wounded taken prisoner, and carried off into Sebastopol. It took a good hours hard and stubborn fighting to drive the enemy off, but they were at last made to retreat leaving the place strewn pretty thickly with their dead. During this affair, we had five men killed and seventeen wounded, but the French loss was much heavier. On the other hand, the Russian loss could not have been less than seven or eight hundred. The number of Russians lying wounded in our trenches and on the field proved that they had received severe chastisement which they most certainly deserved, and they lost quite a number of officers, as well as men.

In our trench, the bodies of one officer and 18 men remained until next day: the ground, was literally covered with their dead. About 10 a.m. a flag of truce was hoisted from the Malakoff when Prince Gortchaskoff asked for an armistice to give them a chance to bury their dead which of course was not refused by Lord Raglan, who gave him from 10 a.m. until 3 p.m. for that purpose. The white flag was at once hoisted on Peels battery and the moment both flags were up, friend and foe swarmed out of their respective batteries and commenced to pick out their comrades and to bear them off the field. It was a strange sight, for notwithstanding all that had occurred, the English, French, and Russians were exchanging civilities just the same as on a previous occasion, laughing and chatting gaily together as if they had only just met on the *boulevards* in Paris for a walk.

In the meantime the work of clearing off the dead and caring for what wounded were still alive, was steadily going on. In some places, a motley group of French, English and Russians had fallen together broken muskets, bayonets, pouches, belts, fragments of tunics and all kind of debris being scattered amongst around them. Broken gabions, fascines, and dilapidated sand bags were visible on all sides whilst the solemn procession of soldiers bearing their comrades to their last resting place looked a melancholy, not to say ghastly spectacle. In the midst of these results of war a certain amount of conversation riot at all of a melancholy tendency was taking place between our men and the Russians, such as "*Bono Inglais!*" "*Français no bono!*" "*Rooso bono!*" leading us to believe that they liked the British soldiers, much better than they did the French which heaven knows they had no great reason for doing for we always made it as hot for them as we knew how and for which they gave us the name of "Red devils."

It must have taken more than three hours to bury the dead, who were laid down gently side by side in one deep, wide pit, when observations something like the following, would escape the lips of a man who recognised a messmate in the gory corpse then beings brought upon the stretcher for interment. "That's poor Peter Abbott!! he was my right hand man!" "There's Dan Sullivan he'll never guy ould Blake about his bald pate again!!" "Look at sergeant Kent! Devil a man he'll ever put in a guard room again! but no matter, he was a good duty sergeant but rather strict. What's the good of all his strictness to him now?" "Oh! poor Andy Hynes, I know him by his red hair! Lord have mercy on his poor soul and may the soil rest lightly over his ashes! He was a good kind hearted creature" and so on.

When the time for truce had expired, the white flags had scarcely disappeared, before a round shot from the sailors' battery, knocked through one of the pillars of the Redan raising a perfect cloud of dust. The Russians were by no means slow to reply and soon war was raging as hard and fast as ever. We were not sorry when our relief arrived that morning for we were considerably depressed at having to bury so many of our brave comrades that day who had fought so gallantly the night previously. But everything in this world is bound to come to an end some time, so the long wearisome day terminated as we were marched to our camp under cover of darkness.

Next day as we were eating our dinner in our tent (if I may be pardoned for so calling it, but I think "*tiffiin*" as the swells say would be the more appropriate term for we had nothing before us that would justify me in dignifying it with that appellation, save our usual rations of hard tack, salt junk and coffee) there walked in one of the Enniskilleners who was employed in dispatch duty on General Pennyfeather's staff, whose tent stood in convenient proximity to ours, and after joining us at our request in some of the good things that were going, lit his pipe sociably and then amused us very much by a thrilling recital of the Battle of Balaklava, in which he had been.

The veracity of more than one incident related so ably by him, was vouched for by the scars he exhibited about his body. One sabre cut had deprived him of his left ear. I will endeavour for the edification of my reader to repeat the story as nearly as I can in the manner in which he told it.

CHAPTER 10

The Enniskillen's Story of Balaklava

If I live a hundred years I shall never forget that memorable morning the 25th of October. Before we had time to water our horses or to eat anything ourselves, which we had not done since the day before, we were alarmed by the trumpet sounding "boot and saddle" and we had no time to surmise what was the matter, when we found ourselves drawn up in squadrons on the slope behind the redoubt in front of our camps. On glancing to the left, we beheld ten or eleven compact columns of Russian cavalry who had just debouched from the narrow mountain passes near the Tchernaya River and were advancing in a determined manner up the plains towards Balaklava covered by regular lines of field batteries of at least 25 or 30 pieces strong. Two batteries of horse artillery were already almost a mile in advance of the remainder and firing with eternal strength on the redoubts which were manned by the timorous Turks, and from which came puffs of smoke at intervals.

Behind these guns were enormous bodies of Russian cavalry. They were massed together in dense, solid columns and advanced *en échelon* towards the Turks. The valley was lit up with the blaze of their sabres, lances, and gay uniforms, green and gold, blue and silver with furred *pelisses*, and jackets richly embroidered on the breast and sleeves and all the glitter of a fine equipment. Their number was something over two thousand five hundred strong. In the front and extended along the intervals between each battery of guns were lines of Cossack skirmishers. The first effect of the enemy's appearance was to cause no end of a commotion amongst the wearers of the turbans and *fez* caps in the redoubt as the shells of the enemy burst over them. The Cossacks advanced rapidly and the Turks at once got completely scared when they saw the overwhelming number of their enemies and after firing a few ineffective shots fell at their approach and then made no more ado, but ran in scattered groups across the plain towards Balaklava, some running down the deep slope and some pitching headlong from the escarpment of the parapet.

But the Cossacks were well mounted and pursuing the fugitives soon overtook them and began to ply lance and sabre to some purpose amongst the flying herd who were knocked over in their flight like ninepins, upsetting each other as they endeavoured to evade their pursuers. As a remnant of them were straggling from the front with their goods and chattels on their backs and occasionally prostrating themselves in the direction of Mecca praying to *Allah* to save them from the ferocious Muscovites, they were intercepted in their flight by three fair Amazons who were employed at a small stream washing linen for the Connaught Rangers.

"Go back and fight for yer counthry, this minute yez cowardly heathens!!" cried the most masculine looking one of the trio and at the same time administered a clout on the ear, with the cloth she was wringing, to the foremost runaway "Start back I tell ye with that in yer lug! Hi! Mrs. Macdonald! Mrs. O'Connell come here an' help me we must stop these flying thieves of the whole world! It's most loikely they have eaten our brave min's dinners as they come by, for ye persave they have their gobs full! Give yon sheepish looking loon a whack wid yer fist Mrs. O'Connell."

"Oy! oy!" replied the latter as she cuffed the gentleman attired in dark blue, baggy nether garments and red *fez* cap.

Meantime, the third damsel, made a brisk and particularly liberal application of the wash board which she had been using.

"*Mashalla!! Mashalla!!*" cried the wicked delinquents. *Whack! whack!* went the clout.

"Sich a disgrace! Give it to 'em the cowardly thieves" shouted the leader of the party whilst the other two emitted screams of revengeful triumph, and continued the onslaught with increased vigour.

"Sure the divils can't be satisfied with one dacent woman for a wife, but must have two or three hundred!"

"Oh divil a lie in it Mrs. O'Connell," said the leader "sure they're no betthor than the Mormons."

"Arrah! now Mrs. Macdonald d'ye tell me so?" said Mrs. O'Connell, after the moslems had made good their escape from the clutches of

1. *The Crimean Campaign With "The Connaught Rangers," 1854-55-56* by Nathaniel Steevens also published by Leonaur.

100

their fair assailants.

"Devil a lie I'm tellin' ye!" said Mrs. Macdonald, "Sure, it wor no later nor last wake that Tim tould me as how these theivin *infidels* can have as many wives as they loike!"

"Oh! the hevins" said Mrs O'Connell, as she turned up the whites of her eyes skywards, "in troth it is meeself that is sorry entoilly that our brave men have to fight fur sich hathens!!"

As the three fair daughters of Erin were debating on the morality of the Turks a dull heavy continuous sound announced the approach of cavalry and almost before they had been aware of it, a numerous body of Cossacks swept past them in the direction of Balaklava.

One glance at the make of their long gray coats and deep saddles and the broad caps was enough to show who and what they were.

"Begorra we'll be taken prisoners av we stay here any longer" exclaimed Mrs O'Connell. "Look! look! at all the Rooshan cavalry crassin the plain"

"Faith! thin asthore machre! it's thrue for ye!" said Mrs Macdonald "let's be off at once, but sure ain't the Hilanders up on Mackenzies heights younder and won't they look after us?"

So saying they collected their clothes and washing utensils and retreated in rear of the Highlanders who had already formed line to defend McKennzies' Heights. The large body of Russian cavalry which at first moved rapidly forward, gradually slackened into a walk as they came crowding on to our front lines. The extreme peril of the moment was impressed upon every one of us as well as those who from their elevated position, saw plainly now that upon our two short lines of dragoons perhaps depended the safety of the base of British operations. We anxiously watched their every movement, waiting in great suspense for the order to dash at them. The very silence was irksome for it was only broken (save by the distant report of big guns), by the champing of their horses bitts and the chink of their sabres in the valley just below us. For a short time the Cossacks walked their horses slowly to allow them to get their breath and then in one grand line they charged in towards Balaklava. The ground seemed to fly under their feet as they gathered speed at every stride and dashed forward in the direction of the Highlanders. With bated breath the occupants of the heights awaited the crash and bursting of that terrible advancing wave upon the line of Gaelic rock, but ere they had come to within two hundred yards, down went that front line of steel and out rang a volley which carried terror and destruction into the heart of the Russians. A second volley caused them to wheel about, open files right and left, by threes about, and then return at a greater pace than they had come; "Well done Highlanders!" exclaimed Sir Colin Campbell, and a hearty cheer from our lusty lungs as well as every spectator, repaid the Highlanders for their gallantry. When we saw them returning, we began to think that we should not be called into action, anxious as we were to go for them, but we were not kept long under that impression, for a second line was advancing on their left at an easy gallop towards the brow of the hill. By this time their numbers had been reinforced by two thousand more who were now seen moving up rapidly to support them.

A perfect forest of lances glistened in the sun as they reached the summit of the little hill. The instant they came in sight, both our trumpets and those of the Grays rang out loud and shrill through the valley and then Lord Cardigan gave the Light Brigade the command, "Charge!!" and with our gallant colonel at our head, away we dashed right at the very centre of the Russian cavalry! Oh! when I think of it and look back at how we rushed at them, I feel more nervous, a great deal, than I did then; for we had no time to think of anything only rushing to the front. As we advanced, the Russian line, brought forward each wing, and at one time threatened to surround and completely annihilate us as we passed on, but they had met their match and more than their match for once in their lives, for as lightening flashes through a thunder cloud, so we pierced through the Russian cavalry. (The Cossacks were commanded by Prince Menchikoff.) The shock was terrible! there was a clash of steel and a light play of swords in the air, and we cut them to pieces all around us.

Yells and shouts burst from the Russians and their pistols were discharged at us, points and cuts exchanged and then we hewed a passage right through their squadrons which shook and quivered before us as we literally rode them down and trampled them under our horses' hoofs. In a few more moments, the spectators saw us emerge and dash on (although diminished in numbers) against the second line, which was advancing against us in the hopes of retrieving the fortunes of the day. The remains of the first line of Russians the majority of whom we had hacked to pieces, had fled off in confusion and general disorder. When a third line came to the rescue it was a fight of heroes and the bravest heroes that ever bled on a field of, battle could have done no more than we did that day by sheer courage and determination.

We and the Grays were winning our way right through the enemy's squadrons, when out to our relief darted the 1st Royal and the 4th and 5th Dragoon Guards who took the enemy in flank, and thoroughly dismayed, away flees the hostile swarms of Muscovites in the wildest retreat, whilst high in the air flashed our heavy swords, which came down with a vengeance and sharp blows fell fast and furious upon Russian heads and shoulders. We perfectly paralyzed the Cossacks who fell into chaos and confusion, so much so that they were obliged to retreat in rear of their artillery columns to endeavour to rally their squadrons in anything like order.

Again we expected that this affair would have capped the climax of the day's proceedings, and so it most likely would have done, for the Russians were in full retreat, only that someone made a great mistake. But who that man was could not be found out, for dead men tell no tales. And now occurred that melancholy disaster so famous in song and history but which filled us all even the spectators with grief. Lord Lucan it appears, being ambitions to recover the guns taken from the Turks gave an order in writing to Captain Nolan, of the Enniskillen Dragoons, to take to Lord Cardigan, directing him to make a charge and recover the guns from the enemy, if possible. After delivering his message, the gallant *aide-de-camp* volunteered to lead the troops in person.

The order was given by Lord Cardigan "Charge!!" and the light cavalry brigade under his command led by Captain Nolan, began to move down the "valley of death" as it has since been called. As they marched towards the front, the Russians opened fire upon them from their field pieces as well as from the guns in the redoubt and also poured in dreadful volleys of musketry.

We saw them plainly as we were drawn up in line just in rear of their position and could scarcely believe our eyes, for it seemed so foolish for a mere handful of cavalry to charge a whole army in position. However such was undoubtedly the fact. Bravely and boldly they swept onwards, glittering in the morning sun, in all the pride and splendid panoply of war. Their desperate valour knew no bounds as on they dashed with on undulating motion that bespoke accelerated pace. Their comrades gazed in sad amazement from the heights behind us.

Oh! if the trumpet would only sound the recall But no! the thought is vain and hopeless. Fate impels them to a dreadful doom which obedience decrees and courage will not evade, and for the honour of "the Flag of Old England" the flag that has braved the battle and the breeze for over a thousand years, that flag that stir? the heart of every Britain at sight of it, they made that desperate charge. A more fearful sight was never witnessed by those, who without the power to aid beheld their heroic countrymen rush into the arms of what seemed inevitable death.

As they crossed the plain the whole line of the enemy belched forth flame through which hissed the messengers of death. Their flight was marked by dead men and horses, wounded or riderless steeds flying in every direction. But they never halted or checked their speed one instant, although their ranks were thinned by round shot and musket balls. With flashing blades whirling above their heads, and with a cheer which was many a brave fellow's death cry, they flew into the batteries, leaving the plain strewed with the bodies of their comrades. Through the clouds of smoke could be seen their sabres flashing, as they rushed up to the guns and dashed between them, cutting down the gunners who crouched beneath gun and limber, behind wheels, and under the gun horses, cleaving their foe to the chin at every stroke.

Brave Captain Nolan dashed through the enemy's ranks backwards cutting them right and left before a bullet laid him low. But there is no time for pausing or ferreting out the foe, and they still fly forward pell-mell for now all is wild excitement, and deadly showers of bullets and cannon shot are forgotten. The Russians appalled by this terrific onslaught, as well they might be, waver before their desperate adversaries, but they cannot pursue beyond a certain distance. Already the foe is circling round to hem in the scattered remains of that brave and noble brigade, and the Russian gunners after the storm of cavalry had passed, returned to their guns. They saw their own cavalry mingled with the British who had just ridden over them, yet they poured in a murderous fire of grape and canister on the struggling mass of men and horses, involving friend and foe in one common ruin.

The decimated heroes returned, very few being untouched. The wild charge had passed over like a tornado leaving traces of devastation and ruin behind. A dreary plain, strewed with the bodies of the wounded, dying and dead. The maimed and mutilated charger, with his military trapping exhibited a horrible spectacle whilst others riderless and untouched galloped to and fro in the most excited manner or stood beside the motionless form of their last owner. Let us now turn away from the sad scene and cry "All honour and glory to the heroes of Balaklava!!" for their desperate chivalry that day saved the British Army, struck fear into the hearts of the enemy and crowned the Light Brigade with a wreath of laurels.

Charge of the Light Brigade.
Blow the bugle! sound the trumpet!
Let the clarion's thrilling cry,
Borne upon the passing breezes,
Speak defiance far and nigh!
Let the ringing echoes wake
The stillness of the autumn day,
Where the little band of horsemen
Wait the signal for the fray!

Few they are, but every breast
Is swelling with a purpose high,
And a stern resolve is flushing
In the light of every eye;
One the thought in every bosom,
One the dearest wish for all,—
If it may not be to conquer,
Yet for Britain's sake to fall!

Blow the bugle! sound the trumpet I
Let the glorious pennons wave,
Gaily floating in the sunlight
O'er the helmets of the brave!
For, at last the word is given.
And, to battle for the right,
See the little band of horsemen
Riding onward to the fight!

Not to snatch an easy triumph.
Not to chase a flying foe.
Not to meet in equal conflict—
Man to man and blow to blow;
Not with any hope of bringing
Proudly back the victory;
But when duty leads them onward.
They are riding forth to die!

For the path of honour lies
Across a long and rugged plain,
Where each onward stride is measured
By the fall of comrade slain.
See the dark and serried masses

Of the foeman far away,
And on either side the cannon
Grimly waiting for their prey!

Blow the bugle! sound the trumpet!
Sound it with a solemn strain;
As the noble British horsemen
Ride across the furrowed plain
Twice three hundred light dragoons
In their pageant and their pride—
Tell me, who, of all that number.
Shall return at eventide?

None of all will play the craven.
None will rein his charger back.
As they press together onward
All along the deadly track.
Fewer still, but still advancing
Till they gain the fatal goal—
Fitting resting-place for heroes,
Where the martial thunders roll!

Oh! how sad, and yet how glorious!
Stretched beneath an eastern sky.
Parted not in direst peril.
Side by side the heroes lie.
Far away from lordly castle,
Far away from country home,
Severed each from many a loved one
By the leagues of ocean foam!

Weep, oh, weep not for the fallen.
Weep not for the young and brave
Doomed in all their grace and beauty
Thus to find a soldiers grave;
For they died the death of heroes,
Died at duty's stern command,
Died for those they loved in Britain,
Fighting in a foreign land!

Say not, 'twas in vain their promise,
Say not that it was in vain—
All the precious life blood shed
So freely on that gory plain!

Come what may—to fail or conquer—
They have nobly done their part.
And their deed of dauntless daring
Strengthens every failing heart.

Speak it not with stern rebuking
To the sordid love of self.
Shames it not their lofty bearing.
Schemes of pleasure or of pelf
Reads it not a lesson to
The lagging soldiers of the cross,
Bidding them to bear unshrinking
Pain and suffering and loss!

Yes, their lofty, proud devotion
Lives enshrined in many a heart,
Nerving many a wavering spirit
To embrace the noble part.
And to fight life's battle bravely.
Till the sounds of discord cease,
And the strife of earthly passions
Fade before the reign of peace!

CHAPTER 11

The Assault on the Redan

Early on the morning of April the 6th, one of our thirteen inch mortar batteries, fired several of their mighty large shells into the Redan, and after they had exploded, we could see large beams of timber, men's bodies arms and legs, blown into the air. One of those shells sunk deep into the earth and exploded a magazine, tearing their earth works to pieces. We could see the blaze of fire run along a portion of their works like lightning.

During the night the working party in the advanced trench, were pounced upon in the middle of the night by the Russians and a regular hand-to-hand conflict ensued A most unlooked for occurrence happened to our men at this juncture, for being armed with the new Enfield rifle they found in many cases that owing to the newness of the wood, the ramrods had become fast, and unable to be withdrawn; the rain having caused the wood to swell and the iron ramrods to become wood-bound. After the first volley therefore, they had no resource, but to use the bayonet and club their rifles, or the bill-hooks, spades, and pick-axes with which they had been working. As soon as the sentries gave the alarm the covering party from the third parallel came to their assistance and after a fierce contest, the Russians were repulsed leaving plenty of dead and wounded behind them.

Our loss on that occasion was thirty men killed and wounded.

The next morning on reaching camp we were agreeably surprised at beholding two wooden huts which had been erected for our regiment during our absence: one for the grenadiers and the other for the light company. On taking possession of these comfortable huts we were very pleased at the change and besides to make things more pleasant, we were receiving a small supply of firewood and altogether the prospect was brighter. The weather too was getting fine and the camp ground dry. We had also got a divisional canteen established, where we were able to purchase a few articles (though we had to pay a high price for them) such as butter, bread, cheese, ale and porter besides several other useful articles which we required to strengthen us after the hardships we had suffered during the cold winter.

We were now getting winter clothing, when we did not need it so much. It was too bad that our men did not get these things during the severity of the winter, but even now they were very thankful for them as they came in useful to wear at night and probably saved many a man's life. We were only sorry that our departed comrades could never share these additions to our comfort. As our neat wooden huts rose up in rows, one after another, we looked sadly on the number of mounds of earth which marked the last resting place of those brave soldiers who had perished in their wet blankets. I have much pleasure in stating that there was not a regiment in the Crimea but had some generous friends in the mother country. Our own regiment received from the ladies in Dublin as well as in Leicestershire many luxuries such as eatables and warm clothing, preserved meats and milk.

It was manifest, that we had left many friends behind who did not forget us though far away, in fact the bountiful kindness of the people at home had most liberally contributed to the wants of the army and there is no doubt but that had they only known sooner of our great needs all these presents would have arrived before: their kindness and generosity will never be forgotten. In anticipation of the coming contest for the possession of Sebastopol, a small contingent of 10,000 Turks had been landed at Balaklava on the 8th of April. They had had a long and difficult march to the front, and were the proud possessors of a brass band, which somewhat astonished the British by playing "Rule Britannia" as they marched past our camps. Some of the regiments were preceded by drums and fifes.

The colonel of each regiment and their two majors rode at the head of their respective corps, mounted on small but spirited horses. Covered with rich saddles cloths: they were followed by their pipe bearers. The mules with the tents marched on the right and the artillery on the left, each gun being drawn by six horses, whilst the baggage animals brought up the rear. The regiments, which were armed with new rifles, marched in columns of sections at quarter distance, all displaying rich standards of gold cloth and coloured flags with star and crescent embroidered on them. Each man carried a pack with a blanket on the top, a small piece of carpet to sit upon and some cooking utensils.

As they passed, they had a very warlike appearance, the realty of which was enhanced by the thunder of the big guns at Sebastopol, and the bursting of shells in the air. Their attire consisted of blue uniforms and red caps with a long tassel hanging down behind therefrom: they pitched their tents on the heights of Inkerman. During the afternoon, our whole division were employed building a fence around the burial ground and placing a gate at the entrance, and whilst doing so, we noticed that our generals of divisions and their staffs, were very active throughout the camp and *aide-de-camp* were continually galloping about with orders, leading us to believe that a desperate struggle for the capture of Sebastopol was imminent. Neither was the French staff idle, as General Pellesier and *aide-de-camp* passed by on their way from Lord Raglan's headquarters where it was evident a council of war had been held but nothing definite had been made known.

From the excitement amongst the staff however, we were in expectation of something of great importance transpiring in the near future. We were not held long in suspense for our expectations were realized on Easter Monday-morning at daybreak, when our whole line of batteries from right to left, both English and French opened fire simultaneously on Sebastopol. The instant the firing commenced, the clouds seemed to have burst with the terrific thunder of the big guns, and , the rain came down in torrents, accompanied by a strong breeze of wind. The atmosphere was so thick that the flashes of the guns were scarcely visible and the gunners must have played at guess work part of the time, as it was quite impossible to see more than a few feet in advance.

The entire camp was enshrouded by a sheet of rain and a Black Sea fog causing it to cut a most miserable figure. The tents had many of them been blown down and the mud was already very deep: the ground being covered with slush. Our batteries were thundering away continuously in regular salvos at the rate of forty shots a minute, but what with the down pour of rain and the thick fog, it was such hard work, that it became necessary for the gunners to slacken fire considerably.

The Russians were taken completely by surprise when our batteries opened such a tremendous fire and some time elapsed before they responded. Lord Raglan, Sir John Campbell, and General Sir William Ayer, as wet and drenching as the day was, posted themselves in their favourite spot at the Greenhill trench, from whence they could get a good view all along the whole line of the batteries. At 5 o'clock the sun set in a dark pall which covered the sky, and caused a pale light to fall upon the masses of curling vapour across the line of the batteries. The outlines of the town were just faintly visible through the smoke and rain and the town itself seemed quivering in the light of the lines of fire around it. The ground beneath was lit up by incessant flashes from the artillery, and long tails of smoke streamed across it, spurting up in thick volumes tinged with fire.

The same evening at sundown our regiment furnished 450 men for the trenches. As we were relieving the 21st and 57th regiments, the Russians opened up a tremendous fire from the batteries, but our gunners made excellent practice and soon succeeded in silencing several of their most troublesome guns, and at every shot, the earth was knocked up out of the enemy's parapet and embrasures and many of their guns were dismantled.

The French had likewise done good service by silencing ten guns on the Flagstaff battery, and inflicting heavy damage on their works. On our side we had peppered the Redan to such good purpose that half the guns had been rendered useless, as well as silencing the Malakoff, Barrack, and Garden batteries. Heavy fire was, notwithstanding, kept up on both sides during the night and there was scarcely any cessation of the roar of cannon. We also discharged a quantity of rockets into the town again setting many of the houses on fire and our mortars were very busy plying all the batteries still in operation with shell. We were greatly exposed to the enemy's fire for we were employed as hard as ever we could labour throwing up earth works, patching up embrasures and platforms and mounting big guns. We had mounted two guns in the second parallel, broken platforms had been replaced and damaged guns surrendered their places to others.

On the evening of April 13th, again the batteries on both sides commenced their terrible duel as usual, and from the way in which the Russians replied to us, it was manifest that they must have exerted themselves in a wonderful manner to repair damages, for they had replaced four or five guns, that we had by our fire rendered of no more value as weapons of war, by others, and repaired broken embrasures and parapets and were fully as ready so far as we could judge, to receive our fire as we were to encounter theirs. The fire did not slacken the whole of the night but if anything increased.

About three o'clock as we were repairing a battery on the left of the second parallel, the Russians opened a fierce fire both of shot and shell. A piece of one of the latter knocked the head off the shoulders of one man bespattering Captain O'Connors' face with his brains. Whilst getting the man's brains washed off his face and clothing, another shell exploded near us a piece of which struck Lieutenant William's and cut his eye right out of his head; Morgan Belton and William Stevens being severely wounded with another piece of the shell. We conveyed all that were wounded, to Green Hill battery where their wounds were attended to by the doctor and after the necessary operations they were conducted to the Hospital. The sailors did not escape scatheless, for although they only worked about forty guns, in the different batteries, they lost more men in proportion to their number than we or any of the siege trains did. About the time that Lieutenant Williams received his wound , they had seventy men killed and wounded.

The sailors in Peels' battery on the right attack had silenced five of the best guns in the Redan, (a most important piece of service), the previous day, but the Russians replaced them during the night and opened fire from them vengefully in the morning. The Redan itself was very much damaged in the right and front face, many of the embrasures having been rendered together with the guns, quite useless, but the enemy worked hard to repair damages all night long. They were so numerous that they could easily spare the men, and besides they had no shot and shell to carry from a distance like we had. Twenty thousand Sardinians now arrived and camped on the plain of Balaklava. They had arrived a few days before and their tents were extremely simple, consisting of four of their lances stuck at the corners and the canvas stretched over and around them. They had with them, their transport horses, mules, carts, and other vehicles and were in fact all ready equipped to take the field. The infantry use a stick and their encampment with its flags flying presented a very martial appearance.

On June 6th at 3 o'clock p. m., the whole of our batteries, encircled Sebastopol once more for the third time and opened a terrible fire on the enemy's works. The English and French were powerful enough and in the best of spirits, only too anxious for a chance of a good charge at the Russians with the bayonet, and everyone felt that the intention of going beyond, what, up to the present had only been a vain bombardment, was a step in the right direction caring not one jot for the risk that they must inevitably encounter. Before going into action Lord Raglan and General Pellesier, together with their staff, rode through the camp and were hailed by deafening cheers and acclamations of both nations. There could have been no doubt on their minds as to the courage of the troops that they commanded.

On June the 7th we began to open our fire and this was kept up for some four hours without intermission. The superiority of our arms over that of the enemy was proved at various points before nightfall, especially on the Redan which was the especial point upon which the sailors concentrated their attention. After dark the fire somewhat slackened on both sides but the same relative advantage was maintained by our artillery. Our batteries continued to fire steadily until daybreak, when it assumed a sudden fury. Until the critical moment arrived this was maintained with the utmost activity. This affair commenced at about 4.30 p. m., when the head of the French attacking columns scrambled up the hills like so many cats on the road to the Mamelon. A rocket was thrown up as a signal to our men, and instantly our small force made a rush at the quarries.

Previously to this, the Mamelon had been stormed by the French. This was situated to the right of the Malakoff. After a hard hand to hand struggle we drove out the Russians, turned round the gabions and commenced to fortify ourselves in our newly acquired position. Sergeant Savage of the 88th Connaught Rangers succeeded in capturing two of the Russian officers whom he conveyed to the trenches, thereby securing his commission as lieutenant. At the time that the French went up the side of the hill to take the Mamelon, the *Zouaves* had not been idle and were soon upon the parapet firing down upon the Russians, It was not long before a flag was seen flying there as a signal for a rallying post.

Up and down it went as the battle raged around it. At last they fairly poured into the place and a fierce hand–to–hand encounter followed, with bayonet, musket or anything that could be laid hold of and after a hard contest for possession the French succeeded in sending the Russians to the right-about. At the same time our men were lighting at the quarries and had repelled five successive attacks of the Muscovites who nevertheless displayed the most daring bravery to maintain possession of their position. During the night, they made repeated attacks upon our men to try and regain their lost ground, but our men steadily defended what they had won and even at the sacrifice of many lives succeeded against superior numbers which were continually being reinforced.

The number of hand-to-hand conflicts that took place were unknown but they must have been many. The fiercest sortie of the enemy occurred about three o'clock in the morning when the whole of the batteries were lit up with a blaze of fire; and storms of shot and shell were thrown from the Redan and other batteries. The position held both by French and English at break of day was very important, and the morning brought out the advantages gained and lost, together with the painful scene of the dead and still suffering victims. On our side we had 180 men and five officers killed and wounded, the French losing about 500 men and officers.

The next day the Russians hoisted a flag of truce (by order of Prince Gortchaskoff) to allow them to bury their dead, which was acknowledged by Lord Raglan. The flag was exhibited from the Malakoff to the Redan, and Flagstaff batteries. Green Hill battery responded with the usual white flag as did Peel's. Considering the grave condition of affairs and the critical position in which the contending armies stood, it was a serious request to make, especially in the middle of a fierce bombardment, and there were not wanting many who inclined to the opinion that it was a ruse, for all who know the Russian nature, know that it is almost an impossibility for a true born Russian to speak the truth, and we regarded it suspiciously as an endeavour to gain time, success, hanging as it did in the balance, might even depend upon a single moment. Our suspicions were not far astray either.

From 10 to 4 p. m., during which time the armistice was granted, no shot was tired upon either side and the dead bodies which strewed the hill in front of the quarries were removed from the field of slaughter.

The enemy had not been idle during this temporary cessation of hostilities but had made good use of their time as indeed we knew that they would, and when the firing recommenced which it did the instant the flags of truce were withdrawn, a few minutes before four o'clock, it was plain that the Malakoff and Redan had both received reinforcements of guns: the Russians, having displayed great artfulness in hiding their working parties. During the night we lost a considerable number of men and had many wounded in our new position, into which the Russians kept pouring grape and canister, from the batteries that flanked the rear of the Redan.

After the contests for the Mamelon and rifle pits on the 8th and 9th, a temporary lull took place in the siege operation which was necessary in order to make preparations for a yet more formidable assault on both the Malakoff and the Redan.

On the morning of the 10th June, a council of war was held at Lord Raglan's headquarters, by all the English, French, and Sardinian

Generals and it was then decided to bombard Sebastopol on the 15th, 16th, and 17th, and to storm it between four and five o'clock on the morning of the 18th. The signal decided upon for the general assault being a rocket fired in the air and the French were then to storm the Malakoff, and when the French flag was seen hoisted from the Malakoff the British were at once to attack the Redan which could not be taken as long as the guns from the Malakoff, were not silenced, the latter being a full moon battery and playing across the plain on the Redan.

On June 18th at 2 o clock in the morning the 4th division under command of Sir John Campbell consisting of the first battalion, the Rifle Brigade, 17th, 20th, 21st, 55th, 57th. 63rd and 68th regiments, was marched down to the twenty-one gun battery on the right attack. At that time the bombardment was raging hotly, a galling fire of shot and shell, grape and canister being exchanged on both sides. As we reached the quarries, the 17th leading, the men got packed closely together and the Russians having the exact range, threw a shell right amongst our men, killing four of them. As we stood there a target for the Russians, waiting for the rocket which was to be the signal from the French, a shell came from the Redan, and struck Sergeant Connell of the grenadier company tearing him into shreds and throwing one of his legs fifty yards off which was found afterwards and identified by the regimental number on his socks.

We had much better have tried to get into the Redan, than to stand there in suspense for our men were falling fast. When the signal rocket was at last thrown up, a hard fight began which lasted for about an hour, the French flag being seen flying from the Malakoff about 6 a.m. No sooner was this seen than the British commenced to storm the Redan. A party was at once told off to carry scaling ladders and woolpacks, the latter were placed upon the field as cover for the riflemen, who were told off to cover the advance of the storming party. Whilst we were in front of the Redan and at least fifty yards away, the French were once more dispossessed of the Malakoff by force of arms, and the daylight being obscured by the smoke of the guns to the number of five hundred, besides between five and six hundred thousand rifles, we were unable to see that the French no longer held possession of the Malakoff.

The Russians having recaptured this battery immediately reversed the guns and turned their fire on the British troops massed on the plains in front of the Redan. As the allied troops advanced to the assault, they were met by a shower of shot, shell, grape and canister, rifle bullets and pieces of old iron, even old nails which were discharged by the Russians from the Redan, besides being harassed by a cross fire from the Malakoff, causing immense slaughter.

Our general Sir John Campbell and our Captain John Croker were killed as we got close up to the Redan. I was close to him in the front rank when he fell. Many of the ladder men were killed and the ladders strewed the field. By dint of perseverance and hard work, the ladders were got as far as the abattis, where there was another delay for during the night the Russians had repaired and strengthened it.

This obstructed the advance of the ladder party who used the greatest exertions to remove that barrier. All who were not shot, worked through and deposited their ladders in the ditch of the Redan.

The storming party consisting of the 17th, 21st, 57th and 63rd regiments including the Rifle brigade attacked the left side of the immense and formidable stronghold. The light Division led by General Brown consisted of the 7th, 23rd, 33rd, 84th, 47th, 77th, 88th and 90th regiments and were situated on the right side, whilst the 2nd Division were in the centre.

Two of my comrades were blown to pieces by the bursting of a shell, in fact men were falling all around me and we could not avoid walking all over them.

During the assault on the Redan and Malakoff the third division under General Sir William Eyre consisting of the 1st Royals, 9th, 18th, 28th, 38th, 46th, 89th and 97th began to move.

At the signal for the general assault, the 18th Royal Irish being the storming party, rushed at the cemetery on the left attack and got possession, dislodging the Russians with small loss.

But the moment the Russians retired, the Barrack, Garden, and Crow's Nest batteries opened a heavy fire upon us which was responded to by our No. 11 battery, which very soon silenced them.

The 18th at once rushed out of the cemetery towards the town and succeeded in getting into some houses, Captain Harris was gallantly leading his company, when he was shot. Once in the houses the men prepared to defend themselves. Meanwhile the enemy did their best to blow them to pieces with shot both grape and canister, but the men kept close though their loss was great. They had entered the houses daring the early part of the day, and were unable to leave them until evening.

The enemy at last blew up a great many of them and set fire to several others. When our men rushed out, the. fire was spreading all over. The 9th also effected a lodgement in some houses and held possession as well as the 18th. It is a grave question, why these men were not supported by adequate bodies of troops so as to enable them to take the enemy in the flank and move round behind the Redan.

This was no fault of the men, neither was it the men's fault that the Redan was not breached by round shot and the abattis swept away, before the assault was made. And the assault being made, whose fault was it that large bodies of troops were not rushed forward to the Redan? It certainly was not the men's, nothing could surpass the daring, bravery, and courage of both officers and soldiers of the British army when they were brought properly into action. But when a mere handful of men were sent to take a stronghold like the Redan, armed as it was with all sorts of engines of destruction and manned by an immense force, it could not be expected that the men could do impossibilities..

At 10 o'clock in the morning of the 19th, an armistice was granted by the Russians to bury the dead and accordingly flags of truce were hoisted on the Redan and Malakoff by order of Prince Gortchakoff which Lord Raglan caused to be answered by Green Hill battery. The time granted was from 10 in the morning until 4 o'clock in the afternoon. In a few minutes after the display of the flags, burying parties of French and English emerged from the trenches and commenced to carry off the dead, burying them all in one grave in the rear of the trenches, just as they had fallen in their clothes. The officers were taken to camp and buried at Cathcarts' Hill. Close to the abattis many wounded men were found some of whom had been lying there thirty-six hours in their blood stained uniforms, beneath the burning sun, without a drop of water to quench their thirst. Some of them had crawled away during the night and hundreds had died of their wounds as they lay.

After the burial was over hostilities recommenced as soon as the white flags disappeared. As the wounded were being born along in streams along the Worondzoff Road, towards the hospital we could not help regretting our loss both of officers and men and especially our own brave Captain John Croker. He was an exceedingly kind gentleman, but a strict officer, who expected every man to do his duty faithfully and zealously. He was most generous and always anxious for the comfort and amusement of his company. A braver, more dignified or gentlemanly officer, or a kinder friend than Captain John Croker, was not to be found in the service, nor was there any more precise, more exacting or more awake to the slightest professional neglect of duty, and his loss to the grenadier company, I am sure was deeply and sorely felt. He was a native of County Limerick.

LINES ON THE DEATH OF SIR JOHN CAMPBELL
AND CAPTAIN JOHN CROKER, WHO FELL,
LEADING THE ASSAULT ON THE GREAT REDAN,
    JUNE 18TH, 1855.

Ye Grenadiers I who fear no foe.
And scoff at death, full well I know.
That to your dying breath.
You'll fight like warriors, or like heroes fall,
So, now, obey your queen and country's call.

To crush those Russians with relentless hand
And scale their rampart, like a gallant band.
Let Sir John Campbells' orders be our guide—
We'll fight and conquer by that hero's side.

Nor will we humble to the Russian Bear:
Whilst God is with us, we need never fear;
Grasp your swords for victory's glorious crown.
And share with none these deeds of high renown.

The warriors brave around John Croker stood
Within the quarries ready to shed their blood;
While our noble captain on the signal given
Cries; "Grenadiers I advance and trust your fate to heaven!"

Strong with desire we raised the battle cry
And rushed well forward to win the fight or die,
Our captain waved high his sword, and then
Onward he dashed followed by all his gallant men.

Who, with one loud hurrah the silence broke
And charged like Britons through the fire and smoke;
A moment more the bloody struggle came
With war of cannon and with flash and flame.

While piled in ghastly heaps brave soldiers lay
Filling the trenches with their dead that day,
Croker's voice was heard above the battle din.
Leading his company through deadly slaughter then.

Until at last the fatal bullet riven

Laid our hero low and sent his soul to heaven
Deep was the grief and sorrow at his loss we bore
As the noble chieftain lay weltering in his gore.

While round his ghastly corse we bravely tried
To quell the sweeping torrent, the rushing tide,
That foamed upon us with resistless ire
And levelled our heroes in heaps—there to expire.

But few escaped of the forlorn band,
Of that chivalric company Croker did command,
But those who did, stuck by their leader still,
And laid his corpse to rest on Cathcart Hill.

CHAPTER 12

The Fall of the Town

The 28th June, 1855, was a day of sadness and regret to the officers and men in camp on learning that Lord Raglan had departed this life at 9 o'clock p. m. His death appeared to still every feeling but that of respect for his memory and the remembrance of the many long years he faithfully and unretiringly served his country, and his frequent cheering visits amongst the men in camp, had endeared him to the whole army A military procession was formed before Sebastopol at 4 o'clock in the afternoon of the 3rd of July, to escort the body to Kamatche Bay. As many as could be spared from duty in the trenches, with safety to the camp, from every infantry regiment, formed an avenue from the British to the French headquarters and thence to Kamatche Bay where the *Ariadne* man-of-war lay ready to receive her melancholy freight. The French troops formed a similar avenue, the cavalry and batteries of artillery were formed up behind the lines of infantry, and bands were stationed at intervals playing the dead march as the procession moved slowly along the route marked out by the line of infantry. The coffin was carried on a gun-carriage, the soldiers hearse, and at each side rode the four commanders of the allied armies. Then followed the generals and officers who could be spared from trench duty.

As the solemn procession moved slowly onward,, minute guns were fired by the field artillery of the French At Kamatche Bay, marines and sailors were formed upon the wharf the naval officers were in attendance and the body of Lord Raglan was placed on board the *Ariadne*.

Thus was he removed from that battlefield where his body and mind had suffered for the last nine months and where many hundreds of gallant officers lie in their gore and glory awaiting the last summons.

On August the 25th, Captain Coulthurst arrived with a draft of 200 men, who were posted to the different companies. We had 25 of them in our company, the grenadiers, to fill up vacancies left by those who fell in battle or died in hospital from the exposure and hardships of the winter.

During the months of July and August, I was attached to the Royal Engineers, and worked with them in the advance works, under a desperate fire, building batteries and throwing up earth works. Our loss in the trenches was very heavy although the results did not pay in point of fame and honour for the hard work performed by the army. Our outworks had approached so near the Russian batteries that our trenches afforded very insufficient protection from the shot, shell, etc., liberally showered upon us by them, and so many of our working party were killed by these deadly missiles, that our list of killed and wounded was greatly increased every twenty four hours.

The engineers and artillery officers now reported everything ready for one last and desperate assault on the fortifications. The hard work done by the Russians to strengthen the Malakoff, Redan, and all other batteries was almost inconceivable. The two former were defended by a formidable abattis of sharpened stakes in front, a parapet thirty feet high, a ditch fifteen feet deep by twenty wide with heavy guns and mortars placed as thickly as the ground could be covered with them: this is a good description of these strongholds.

The general plan of assault was a vigorous fire to be opened by the allies on the 5th, 6th, and 7th, followed on the 8th of September 1855, by the storming of the Malakoff by the French, and of the Redan by the British. General Wyndham (who succeeded Lord Raglan, to the command of the British army) and Pellessier, arranged that at dawn on the 8th, the French storming columns were to leave the trenches, the British to storm the Redan.

The "Tricolour" flag planted on the Malakoff was to be the signal that the French had triumphed and the British were then to storm the Redan, for unless the Malakoff was first captured, the Redan could not be held, as the former was the key to the position, therefore the Malakoff must be attacked first and with a very strong force. That final bombardment of Sebastopol was simply appalling! It began between 11 and 12 as previously arranged by the commanders who had altered the hour of attack secretly, and unsuspected by the Russians who had fully expected it to occur in the early morning.

The continued firing of shot, shell, etc., shook the very ground owing to the tremendous reverberations of the heavy ordnance, raising clouds of earth and overturning batteries all along the Russian Line; two thousand cannonades and fifty thousand rifles filling the air with vivid sparks and gleams.

The very daylight was obscured and a black pall seemed to settle over everywhere rendering it as dark as night, from the volumes of smoke, and death and destruction was going on all around.

By this time the guns were too hot to put the hand on, and the rifles could be bent, they were so overheated. They however continued with such effect that they cut up all the Russian earth works, but without showing any actual gaps or breaches, which would have been the case, had the batteries been built of stone, under such a heavy fire of shot, shell, grape and canister. This proved without a doubt, the superior defensive power of earth works. All the darkness did not stay this devastation, for every kind of missile continued to fly through the air, leaving a bright line to mark its passage, and bursting and cracking as they crashed against the defences and buildings.

Both the Redan and Malakoff, when no longer visible in daylight, were brought out into vivid relief by the bursting of shells and the flashing of guns. One rocket struck a ship in the harbour and set it on fire and it was burnt to the water's edge. All through the night we kept up a fire on the Russians which effectually prevented them from repairing their parapets and embrasures and with the dawn of day on the 6th the roar of cannon was only interrupted by a few intervals to cool the guns. The enemy instinctively feeling that the hour of peril had arrived, used the greatest exertions to work their batteries. There was unusual agitation visible amongst, them several movements seeming to indicate that they were moving their valuables and all such persons who would not be required to render assistance in the defence, to the north side of the harbour.

Another night of terrible firing ensued and on the 7th there was another ship in the harbour set on fire by one of our rockets, sharing the fate of the former one. Flames now broke out in the town, and all at once there was a loud explosion, like that of a magazine: this occurred in the evening.

On the morning of the 8th, a destructive storm of shot and shell continued until noon, when the French issued forth, preceded by riflemen, sappers, and miners. As a substitute for ladders, the French carried light bridges by which they crossed the ditch and then scaled the parapet with surprising alacrity. The great struggle now commenced with guns, pistols rifles, swords, bayonets, gun-rammers, and anything that could be laid hold of in fact, but in the course of about an hour's time the "Tricolour" floated from the Malakoff announcing that the formidable position was taken. Although the French had captured it, the Russians so well knew its value, (it being the key to the whole position), that they made the most furious attempts at recapture, but the French general judiciously sent powerful reserves to the support of McMahon (then in possession) and these maintained a series of desperate battles against the Russians bayonet, against bayonet, musket against musket and man against man, the combat continuing for several hours.

But the French triumphed and drove the enemy from their stronghold. Anything more wildly disorderly than the interior of the Malakoff appeared, can hardly be imagined. The shells, as they exploded, had turn up the earth, and every part of the ground became a frightful scene of bloody struggles, thousands of the dead and wounded being heaped up within this one fort alone. No sooner was the tricolour seen floating above the Malakoff then General Wyndham gave the signal for the British to storm the Redan, and immediately, out rushed the storming party preceded by those detailed to carry the ladders and the covering party: a mere handful of men altogether.

It appears truly astonishing that so few should have been told off for so great a work. Every soldier had a perilous duty assigned to him; the riflemen were to cover the advance of the ladder party, by shooting down the gunners at the embrasures of the Redan, the ladder party to place the ladders in the ditch, as soon as the storming party rushed from the quarries. The guns of the Redan opened a fierce fire on them the moment they made their appearance, sweeping them down as they advanced.

Colonel Unett, of the 19th regiment, was one of the first officers that fell and brigadier Shirley was wounded; the colonel of the 57th regiment together with Captain Thomas and Captain Harris, of the first battalion of rifle brigade were killed. Indeed scarcely an officer who advanced with the storming party, was not either killed or wounded The distance from the Redan to the quarries was too great, being over two hundred yards, which gave the enemy a good opportunity of mowing the storming party down like grass by a tremendous fire of shot shell, grape, canister and musketry, and when Gotchaskoff saw that the Malakoff was taken, he brought all his reinforcements against us.

The survivors however advanced and reached the abattis, the pointed stakes of which standing outward presented a formidable obstacle to further progress. Nevertheless the men made gaps through which they crawled.

Then ensued another rush for the ditch, when the ladders were found to be too short, but our men scrambled and climbed up, many falling all the time under the shot of the enemy. Officers and men were rivalling each other for the honour of being among the first to enter this tremendous battery, but alas! they were too weak in numbers for such an enterprise. Mounting the parapet, the besiegers saw the interior of the Redan before them filled with masses of soldiers and powerful ranges of big guns and mortars. Wild and bloody was the scene we gazed upon, and no sooner did we gain the interior, that the British flag was at once hoisted.

Captain Williams and the other officers and men did all in their power to dislodge the Russians from behind the traverse and breastworks but after more than an hour's hard fighting they overpowered the handful of men sent to take that stronghold, for we had no support to back up those men that had already, obtained a foothold in the Redan. In the meanwhile, the Russians continued to bring up reinforcements and consequently it was impossible for the British to make headway against them, and we now saw that we must either retreat, or stay to be shot down. New supporting parties kept coming in such driblets and in such confusion, as rendered impossible any well-directed charge against the place.

If for a time a few men were collected in a body volleys of musketry and cannon shots of all descriptions, old pieces of iron, etc., fired from the enemies large guns levelled our men to the dust. Finding at last, that there were no supports coming to their aid, officers and men, lost heart, and retreated to their trenches for we were very glad to get out of the shower of fire. The embrasures of the parapets, the ditch and all around had become a harrowing scene of slaughter, dead and wounded being visible in all directions. Files of them lay at the bottom of the ditch where they had fallen by the Russian shot as they were in the act of climbing up the scaling ladders.

At two o'clock the attack was over, and in the previous two hours, the British loss was very severe.

No other day throughout the war, recorded so many killed and wounded, which amounted to the large number of 1300. The French loss was much greater than ours. The firing was kept up by the Russians until about 12 p.m. when it began to slacken and finally ceased altogether.

At this time, all the British troops were entrenched awaiting to make another attack in the morning. Our batteries began to open a heavy fire at about 4 a. m,. but rather to our surprise we got no response.

It appears as we found out later that Prince Gortchaskoff finding his last hope gone when the Malakoff was taken, determined upon evacuating the Redan and the Malakoff which he did by means of the pontoon bridge, retreating with four hundred thousand troops to the north side. Before leaving Sebastopol however he caused fire to be set to a number of houses and commenced blowing up all the principal buildings in the town as well as the magazines. Lurid flames rose on all sides and explosion after explosion shook the earth causing a good deal of consternation amongst our men in the trenches. The ground behind the Redan was torn up for a great distance by the successive explosions which succeeded each other so rapidly that the air was filled with a thick murky smoke, mingled with flames from the burning buildings, which imparted an awfull grandeur to the scene.

Now the Flag-staff Battery was blown up with resistless violence; a minute or two later and another explosion destroyed the Garden battery and as daylight approached, Fort Paul, Fort Nicholas, Central and Quarantine bastion were seen to be in flames. At the same time the fleet of the Russians, lying in the harbour was sunk. We could not help admiring the manner in which Gortchaskoff carried out his desperate plan: the last available means of saving the remains of the garrison.

It was on the morning of the 9th of September that the troops heard the announcement that the mighty city had fallen! That city which for nearly two years had been looked at and studied by our generals and engineers and in front of which so many of our troops had been killed or wounded. on the preceding day. We could hardly credit the news, so accustomed had all been to the constant dashing of our hopes and the non-fulfilment of happy predictions. All that day we were very busily engaged in burying the dead.

The French soldiers rushed into the town at once, looked about the burning houses and plundered them of all the valuable articles that they could find and carry back to camp with them. They were always on the lookout for plunder, but our men had strict orders not to touch a thing. We had a line of cavalry and provost-marshals all around the town, to stop any person from taking anything out of it.

I may say here that the town was divided into two, half being in possession of the British and the other half being in that of the French consequently they could only loot their own half. When the allied commanders found that the Russian garrison, together with the inhabitants of the town had vacated it they ordered the sappers and miners (whose duty it was) to ascertain whether any traps or explosive mines had been laid by the enemy before our troops were allowed to occupy it, and to ward off camp followers, to divide the spoils of the garrison between the two invading armies, and also to take measures for the destruction of the forts and docks.

The appearance of the town at the time that we entered it was indeed frightful. Destructive forces had been raging with a fearful violence never before equalled in the history of sieges. I went into St Paul's Church, which was the largest structure in the town and oh! what a scene met my eyes! All the rich ornaments and everything within was destroyed by the shell that had come through the roof.

The whole internal area, was a heap of shot pierced buildings, crumbling earth works, torn up streets, broken muskets and guns. We came across many proofs that the Russians had intended to defend the town, street by street, had we forced an entrance, for across every street were constructed barricades defended by field pieces.

In some of the finest houses, there were beautiful pictures. *Bric-à-brac*, and elegant furniture crushed and broken and mingled with the dust on the floor; our 13 inch shells had had a most dreadful effect.

These fearful missiles, of which there were so many thousands thrown into the town, weigh 200 lbs each and when they fall from a height, they have the force of fifty tons, and descending deeply into the foundations of a house, when they explode they scatter everything about, far and near.

Our army still continued to camp outside the town, sending only as many troops as would suffice to guard it, which took possession of some of the best houses still standing and converted them into guardhouses. We could now get plenty of fuel from the town and our fatigue parties could be seen by the Russians from the north side pulling down houses to get at the wood they contained and carrying it to camp. Whilst so engaged the Russians invariably fired upon us from their position which they had strengthened by throwing up very strong forts, armed with their heaviest guns. They had placed some of these guns with the breach sunk into the ground in order to get sufficient elevation and increase the force of the shot.

They would throw a 10 inch shell right into our camp amongst our men. These we called "long rangers "and they did considerable mischief upsetting our tents and not unfrequently killing and wounding some of our men. We had regular guards and sentries all over Sebastopol. As we entered some of the houses, we were horrified to find that some of the dead bodies had not yet been buried: these we threw in the harbour.

On the 15th September I was ordered to join the Royal Engineers and subsequently worked with them blowing up the Government docks and buildings in Sebastopol.

During the time we were engaged in undermining the docks and blowing them up we were much annoyed by the Russians who were continually firing at us. When we had finished our work we were removed to Balaklava, for the purpose of building wharves and making roads at that harbour, for landing and transporting provisions. We had no trench duty to perform, nothing but the regular camp guards, whilst the officers amused themselves by riding races and other sports. We had plenty of fuel and good rations and there were any amount of canteens on the ground so that we were able to make up for the hard times of the winter. The army had nothing to do but make roads all through the camp and was in splendid condition.

The commanders however began to look forward to a second wintering in the Crimea as a probability, and invaluable as the railway had become it was found to be inadequate to the conveyance of the immense bulk and weight of supplies required day by day for the army and hence it became necessary to do that which if done earlier last winter, would have saved many lives *viz*: to make a new road from Balaklava to the camp. The road was accordingly laid out and large bodies of our men worked on it daily, but making roads is but child's play compared to digging trenches under a continual fire of shot, shell, grape and canister.

The whole of the divisions were kept continually upon the road, which promised to be a great success, and we were all anxious to make it so. We had from four to five thousand men employed in this way, between Balaklava and the front.

About the 10th November, this most excellent road was completed and the French at the same time constructed a railway across the valley which connected their camp with Kamiesch Bay; they also improved the old Tartar roads.

Our army suffered much the last winter from a lack of travelling facilities, but this beautiful road, constructed by the British Army, will ever remain as a monuments of their occupation.

During the two weeks in September, which followed the evacuation of the south side of Sebastopol, the. Russians were quietly but actively strengthening their fortifications on the north side, making all the heights bristle with guns and firing a shot whenever an opportunity presented itself to work some mischief upon our guards, sentries, and fatigue parties in the town.

We had erected a few batteries on the northern, heights of Inkerman, so as to remind them that we were ready for them at any minute. Some camp rumours arose concerning some supposed expeditions to Odessa, Nicholoff and other sea port towns on the Black Sea, in Southern Russia, but the securing of the captured city was regarded at the first duty.

On the 20th of September 1855, the anniversary of the Battle of the Alma, a distribution of the medals for the Crimea, and clasps for Alma, Balaklava, and Inkerman, took place amongst the troops of the allied armies. These decorations were much appreciated both by the officers and men, and the day was commemorated with much festivity and amusement in both camps.

On the 1st of October, I received orders at Balaklava to join my regiment which was to go on the Black Sea expedition recently decided upon by the allies.

On the 1st of October the Black Sea fleet were in readiness at Kamiesch Bay, to convey 15,000 of the allied army. The 4th division consisting of 1st Battalion Rifle brigade, the 17th, 20th, 21st, 55th, 57th, 63rd and 68th, together with marines, two batteries of artillery and two companies of Royal sappers and miners, under the command of General Spencer, were embarked on board the fleet by small steam tenders. My regiment had the honour of being conveyed to Kinburn on the *Royal Albert*, Admiral Lines' flagship. The troop having been put on board and everything being ready, we set sail accompanied by several line-of-battle ships, small steamers, gun boats mortar vessels and two French floating batteries which constituted an armament of great magnitude. The English squadron comprised four steam line-of-battle ships, fifteen steam frigates, eight gun boats, four mortar vessels and two steam tenders.

The Russians, who were gathered on the shores of the Black Sea, north of Sebastopol to the number of several thousands, were wild with excitement when this large squadron appeared, but the ships soon disappeared from the Crimea, for Admiral Lines, signalled the several captains to cast anchor off Odessa. As we got out to sea, the bands discoursed music whilst the officers were at dinner. Before dinner they played as usual "The Roast Beef of Old England," which we had not heard for a long time before. As we had no hammocks, we were forced to lay all around the decks in groups during the night.

On the morning of the 10th, we cast anchor at the place appointed by the admiral. It was then the citizen's turn to be alarmed by this display of force. The Russians on the heights in barracks, squares, and all along the quays, became excessively active in making constant observations. We could see the old fashioned telegraph on the towers along the coast working, and crowds of Cossacks, infantry, and artillery formed up along the cliffs ready to defend the place if attacked. All day on the 10th, 11th, and 12th, this was done in order to draw their troops from the neighbouring districts. I may mention here that the flagship *Royal Albert* was a three decker, carry 131 guns.

About 40 French and English vessels forming a line about two miles in length were eagerly watched from the cliffs by large masses of troops.. The rocket boats, gun boats, mortar vessels, and floating batteries might have gone nearer and crumbled the city to ruins, but as it was not our orders, not a shot was fired and thus Odessa was spared for the third time during the war. In the afternoon of the 13th, the squadron weighed anchor, and we arrived at Kinburn on the morning of the 15th. The troops were landed on the beach out of range of the garrison, by the ships' launches.

Each was filled with soldiers and made secure to the other by means of the painter. When the troops had all been got into the launches, they formed several long lines of red coats in little boats each being steered by a naval officer. The first boat of the line was made fast to a small steam tug and the whole were then towed in front of the beach, where we were to land. As the tug ran in towards the shore, she cast off the line of boats and whilst they were still under weigh, each let go the painter and headed towards the beach, coming in close, on a sandy bottom.

The troops at once jumped ashore, and deployed from where we landed to the River Dnieper, whilst the gun boats went up the stream. Two regiments formed an advance guard, *viz*:

The 1st Batalion of the Rifle Brigade, under the command of Colonel Lord Russell, and one battalion of the Algiers Rifles. The fleet drew up in front of the garrison and opened a bombardment, and about 8 o'clock, the artillery opened a heavy fire on the fort. The *Royal Albert, Algiers, Ariadne, Princess Royal, Agamemnon*, and four other ships of the line, assisted by the French fleet approached abreast of the principal fort, the *Sphinx* and *Tribune* attacking the earthworks battery and the *Dauntlers, Hannibal*, and *Terrible*, took up position opposite the battery near the end of the fort, whilst the smaller vessels did *ditto* on the east . and centre of the garrison. After the advance guard had been sent out, we were set to work to cut a trench, from where we landed to the river Dnieper, a distance of about four miles. Whilst we were employed in digging the trench during the day, the advance guard had a skirmish with the Cossacks and compelled them to retreat at the gallop.

The chief labour was the landing of artillery and ammunition. A camp was formed without tents, at four o'clock in the morning at which time we had the trench all finished and manned ready to receive the Russian reinforcements for the garrison, which were expected, but did not arrive. On the appointed morning, the Cossacks were advancing and the guard opened a heavy fire on them, forcing them to retire quicker than they came. Generals Spencer and Bazaine, made a cavalry reconnaissance at daybreak when the Cossacks retired altogether. The bombardment however still went on, thousands of shot, shell and rockets dropping into the fortress and causing a great number of explosions.

On the morning of the 17th a rocket from the *Royal Albert* set fire to the draw-bridge which led into the garrison.

On the afternoon of the 17th of October, Governor Scofflog hoisted a flag of truce on the citadel, which was answered by General Simpson. As soon as the white flag was flown, the fleet ceased firing and the governor forthwith tendered his surrender to General Simpson in military form, by giving up his sword, but not without a passionate exclamation intended to wound national and professional honour. The officers were deeply mortified, and many of them were on the verge of mutiny against the governor, so strongly did they resist any proposals of surrender. The garrison laid down their arms and were marched outside the town and placed close to our camp with a chain of our sentries as well as those of the French around them. The number of prisoners taken was about 5,000, besides a great many killed and wounded. The majority of them were Russian Poles.

Our doctors attended to their wounds in the fort. The governor and prisoners of war were sent off to Constantinople on board of Her Majesty's steamships.

The captors proceeded to garrison Kinburn, repairing and increasing the defences, restoring the walls and embrasures, strengthening the parapets and casements completing efficient barracks and magazines in the interior of the fort and depositing a large amount of military stores of all kinds. When the small garrison on the other side of the estuary opposite Kinburn found that their guns could effect but little against the invaders and that Kinburn was forced to yield, they blew up St. Nicholas fort on the morning of the 18th, and retired a few hours afterwards. On the 20th Generals Simpson and Bazaine, set out on a reconnaissance with about 10,000 men of the allied armies. The first battalion of the Algiers rifles forming the advanced guard in front of the main body.

After marching about twenty miles on a sandy place, which was like a desert, we halted close to a village, piled arms and were allowed to go foraging. Although the town was deserted, the inhabitants had left plenty of provisions, geese, turkeys, pigs and pails of milk were there in abundance, as well as several other articles, which we found useful, besides plenty of vegetables in the different gardens. We divided the town with the French as before. After tearing down some of the houses for camp fuel, we obtained quantities of flour and wheat from the wind mills and as soon as our fire was lighted we commenced cooking the provender on hand.

Whilst some went through the village killing geese, pigs, etc., others proceeded to cut down branches of trees for the purpose of building huts to protect us for the night, covering them with hay and shaking down plenty inside to lie upon, for we had no tents. Every mess erected one of these huts. After indulging in the good things which we found, and enjoying them to our heart's content, we lay down comfortably for the night, making as usual pillows of our knapsacks and having our rifles and side-arms beside us, ready to turn out at a moment's notice. Next morning at 8 o'clock after having had breakfast, we marched 20 miles to an inland town named Padrewsky and halted in front of it. As usual it was divided between the French and English.

About halfway between Padrewsky and this town, we came across the dwelling of a very rich man who run up a flag of truce on his house, and surrendered himself to Colonel Lord Russell, the commander of the advanced guard, who immediately placed sentries all around the premises on which were situated several windmills, etc.

When the main body arrived under command of General Simpson, that gallant general, at once strengthened the guard already stationed, in order to prevent the place from being molested, thus showing the magnanimity of the British, a quality they have always been noted for. The people of the town had fled before our arrival, leaving everything behind them, including bread, butter, milk fowls, etc. As the live stock were killed we brought them into camp. We then set fire to all the Government buildings, which were stored with provisions, intended to be sent to Odessa, for the use of the army. After ransacking the whole place we camped there that night, and on the following day we marched twenty-five miles to the next inland town.

On the 21st of October we commenced the return journey to Kinburn, our haversacks containing quite as much provision as each man cared to carry, which had been obtained at the town.

On the 25th October, Generals Simpson and Bazaine together with the two admirals, held a council of war and it was decided to blow up all the Government buildings and all important places which was accordingly done on the 26th and 27th, everything being completely destroyed in the garrison. The winter now coming on us, it was decided by the heads of the armies to return to the Crimea as we were without tents, and in pursuance of orders received, were embarked on board the fleet from the wharf, at Kinburn. The 17th regiment were conveyed by the *Terrible* which carried 26 guns, all 68 pounders!

She was a paddle boat of light draught enabling her to run into shallow water and chase the Russians into port. The Russian admiral christened her "The Black Sea Cat" from the rapidity of her movements and the accuracy with which she was handled. This magnificent fleet sailing in line, with the two flag-ships leading, signalling their orders to the various captains of the other ships, presented an imposing spectacle, the line extending about two miles. We could not help wondering what the Russians along the coast, must have thought of this immense armament. The fleet cast anchor on the 3rd of November in Kamiesche Bay, and the troops disembarked at once, and marched to our old camp on Cathcart's Hill. That night we laid ourselves down in our huts, and were able to undress, being the first time for a month.

We enjoyed a good sleep which we stood in great need of and the next day we were received by General Wyndham on the grand parade. He congratulated us on the Black Sea expedition which he declared to have been a complete success, and then called for three cheers for

Her Majesty the Queen which were given with a right good will. After this he gave the 4th division, three day's holidays and then told the commanding officers to march their regiments to camp. Amongst other improvements which were made to meet the wants of the army, was a large reservoir in the ravine between the second light and the 4th division constructed by the Royal Engineers and filled by a spring at the foot of Cathcart's Hill. This reservoir was capable of supplying 50,000 troops with water in abundance both summer and winter.

In fact, everything was done to meet the requirements of the army, during the coming winter. There were all kinds of supplies in abundance and we were in the best of health and spirits.

On the 10th November, I was ordered by the orderly sergeant to proceed to Balaklava to join the Royal sappers and miners who were building wharves for the ships to discharge their cargoes. I worked with them until the 26th February, when I received orders to rejoin my regiment at Cathcart's Hill. At the end of February 1856, the diplomatists at Vienna, agreed upon an armistice for the discussion of a treaty of peace and its immediate effect was observable in the Crimea. As soon as the commanders had received information on the morning of the 1st March a white flag was hoisted on the northern heights opposite Inkerman by order of Prince Gotchaskoff, and near it assembled the Russian commanders with their staffs, and the commanders of the allied armies and their staffs. The latter descended across the valley where they met the Russians with whom they discussed the details of an armistice.

The hostilities were to cease for one month during the consideration of the treaty. The quietest month that the allied armies spent in the Crimea was that of March 1856. Although actual hostilities had entirely stopped none of us could say when they were likely to recommence, with ail their horrors. The Vienna diplomatists had only one month to decide the question of peace or war. The commanding officers whilst maintaining their boundary arrangements, did not prohibit the opposing armies having friendly meetings on their respective banks of the boundary line, where both officers and men frequently assembled to look at each other. This intercourse was kept up with peace and friendliness all through the month of armistice. All the divisions had general parades and marching out.

April brought with it the treaty of peace, and in fact before the end of the month when the armistice would have ceased, news was brought by the European ambassadors that it had been signed at Vienna. When the intelligence was communicated, it was decided by the two commanders-in-chief to have a holiday and to fire a Royal salute. The Russians fired 21 guns from the heights over the Tchernaya River and the British also fired 21 guns from the battery on the north, side of Inkerman heights. After the salutes were over, the Russian soldiers came over to our camp and some of our men, those of good character could get a pass over to the north side. Myself and a comrade were granted a pass, and we spent the day with the Russians, who treated us very kindly. The Russians visited our camp daily in large bodies.

Oh the 18th of April 1856, the allied troops had a grand review on the plain of Balaklava. one of the largest plains in the world. We were inspected by Prince Gortschakoff, the commander-in-chief of the Russian Army. We were formed up in a continuous line at quarter column distance on No. 1, the 8th regiment, officers and colours in front. Prince Gortschakoff arrived with his staff and accompanied by a strong body guard of Cossacks, who however came to a halt and arrived on the right of the line. He, together with the commanders of the allied armies, all accompanied by their respective staffs then rode along the line. As he was passing the 68th Light Infantry, (a Yorkshire regiment,) he remarked, "That's the regiment that took the arm off of me at Inkerman!" The band of each regiment played as the commanders were passed in quick time. The number of troops comprising English, French and Sardinians (of whom there were 15,000) was 175,000. Each regiment passed in grand division style, with its band playing in front.

After Prince Gortschakoff had inspected us, he gave the troops great praise for their appearance saying we looked like men made of steel and then he and his generals, took off their hats and gave three cheers for the allied armies. Duties of a more serious nature however now demanded the attendance of the generals. Large armies were to be removed from the Crimea together with vast stores of provisions and ammunition besides all the round shot fired at us by the Russians, together with the guns taken during the siege and assaults, the former of which we had gathered and carried on our backs to the railway *depôt*, from whence they, as well as the guns, were shipped for England. All the commissariat stores too, were brought down from each divisional *depôt* where they had been collected in immense quantities day after day during the summer months.

The orders were given for the various regiments to leave the Crimea, some for the Mediterranean station some for India, and some for South Africa. Some were sent home to England, my regiment being ordered to British North America. All the camp, equipages and stores for each regiment, had to be brought into transport order, and everything carried to Balaklava for shipment. About the 10th May, the 17th regiment, marched from their old camp on Cathcart s Hill and embarked at Balaklava. at two o'clock in the afternoon on board of the Sir Robert Lowe.

At 3 p. m., we moved out slowly between the rocks which over-hang the narrow entrance to the harbour. We were on deck with tearful eyes, taking a last look towards Cathcart's Hill, where we had left so many noble comrades in that cold and desolate plateau, far away from friends and relations. These thoughts filled us with grief as our ship glided through the beautiful calm black waters of the Black Sea, but the land soon faded from our view and we then turned our thoughts homewards, thanking God for the great mercy he had shown in bringing us safely through all the death struggles and terrible hard-ships that our troops had undergone. Truly we had many reasons, to be thankful that we were returning alive and in good health.

The weather being fine, we made the passage across the Black Sea in three days. The fourth day we entered the Bosphorous and later on came to anchor at Constantinople, opposite the *sultan's* palace which saluted us by dipping her flags, from whence, all along the shores we were greeted with deafening cheers. Moreover swarms of pleasure boats came alongside filled with Turkish nobility who threw up a perfect shower of bouquets on the deck of the troop ship, the ships in the harbour, at the same time, saluting us right royally.

After taking a last look at this splendid city, where we had been anchored about five hours, with its beautiful sights, scenery, and envi-ronments, we steamed down the Marmora, passing the Seven Towers on our left and slowly the grand old city faded from view.

We had now entered the Dardanelles after a smooth passage across the sea of Marmora. Nothing could surpass the grandeur of the scen-ery exhibited on both sides of these Straits.

About 2 p. m., we passed the city of Gallipoli where as in the pre-vious cities, thousands of Turks cheered and otherwise showed their appreciation and admiration of the British troops.

On the 13th May, early in the evening, our ship running down the Mediterranean Sea at a good rate, an alarm of fire came from the cook's galley. The troops were immediately formed up along the decks and the pumps manned. After half an hour's hard work we succeeded in mastering the fire before it had done much harm; another instance of the bravery of the British troops in an emergency of great danger. Had the fire been less promptly and coolly dealt with the consequences might have been very serious considering the number of people on board. On the morning of the 18th May, we arrived at Malta and were then transferred to the *Vulcan* one of Her Majesty's men-of-war which carried 84 guns. We left Malta two days later and on the morning of the 24th May, we sighted the Rock of Gibraltar rearing its lofty crest to the sky. As we rounded Europa Point our ship hoisted her number, (every ship that passes the Rock, must show her colours) which was answered from the signal station, standing on the loftiest point of the Rock.

At 4 o'clock we cast anchor in the harbour. Many of our old friends came on board and welcomed us back from the Crimea. We were also rejoiced to see them and our old station once more. We left Gibraltar on the morning of the 26th, fine weather prevailing and a stiff breeze coping through the straits, leaving the high mountains of Africa behind us on our left and the mountains of Spain on our right.

On the morning of the 28th May the engine of our ship broke down as we were steaming across the calm waters of Trafalgar Bay. The mail coming from the East fortunately just at that time, our captain signalled her and she at once came to our assistance and towed us back to Gibraltar where we remained 17 days, getting our engine repaired. On the 14th June we again left Gibraltar and after a very rough passage across the Atlantic, arrived at Halifax on the 15th July. After staying there two or three days we set out for Quebec on the 22nd July 1856 our voyage having been somewhat delayed by being obliged to anchor every night on account of the large size of our ship. The citizens received us with great courtesy and tendered as a grand dinner in the Citadel.

On the 26th I was sent to Point Levis on outpost duty to prevent desertion to the United States.

In April 1858 our regiment got the route for Montreal. We left Quebec on the 10th arriving in Montreal on the 11th. We took up our quarters in the old Quebec Barracks. On the 15th I was sent to St. Annes as corporal in command of a lookout party.

On the 10th June 1859, I joined my regiment in Montreal and took charge of the regimental police.

In the spring of 1860 our regiment got the route for Quebec, when, we arrived there we took up our quarters in the Citadel.

In June 1862, I obtained my discharge after ten years service and settled in this country where I have since remained, not forgotten by my country.

My Own, My Native Land.
Where'ere I roam, whatever realms to see,
My heart untravelled fondly turns to thee
Such is the patriots' boast, where'ere we roam
His first best country, e'er is at home
And trembling, shrinking from the spoiler's hand,
Far, far, away thy children leave the land
Ill fares the land to hastening ills a prey.
Where wealth accumulates and men decay
Princes and lords may flourish or many fade,
As breath may make them as a breath has made
But a bold peasantry, their country's pride
When once destroyed, can never be supplied
A time there was ere Irelands' grief began
When every rood of ground maintained its man
For him light labour spread her wholesome store
Just gave what life required, but gave no more
His best companions innocence and health
And his best riches, ignorance of wealth
The broken soldier kindly bade to stay
Sat by the fire, and talked the night away
Wept over his wounds or tales of sorrow done
Shouldered his staff and showed how fields were won.

www.ingramcontent.com/pod-product-compliance
Lightning Source LLC
Chambersburg PA
CBHW021010090426
42738CB00007B/737